Sophie
An Edwardian Childhood

First published 2012
by Musisca Publishing, Topsham, Exeter.
Designed by Julia Harris
Printed in Great Britain by
Short Run Press Limited, Exeter

Copyright © Philippe Oboussier 2012

All Rights reserved.
No part of this publication may be reproduced,
stored in any form or by any
means, electronic, mechanical, photocopying,
recording or otherwise without the prior
permission of the copyright owner.

ISBN 978 0 9575219 0 2

All illustrations unless attributed in their
accompanying caption to another artist are
the work of Sophie Leighton Harding.

The originals of all photographs and
illustrations in this book are the property of
Sophie Harding's surviving family.

This book is dedicated to the memory of Sophie's daughter,
my dear wife Caroline Oboussier (1928 - 2007)

Philippe Oboussier

Thanks go to Lily Neal, Robert and Lynnie Harding,
Amanda Davey, Andrew David and Caradoc Doy, all of whom have
contributed to the production of this book.

Sophie at the age of four, painted by her father

Sophie
An Edwardian Childhood

Sophie Leighton Harding

How I Became a Painter's Child

… One

HOW I BECAME A PAINTER'S CHILD

My name is Sophie Blair Leighton and, although it may seem incredible to you, I was born more than a hundred years ago. My mother gave birth to me in 1902, the year after Queen Victoria died. In this picture I am about seven years old and you can see me with my favourite bears, who were clearly on best behaviour for the occasion.

Funnily enough, I remember the photograph being taken because I was very uncomfortable sitting on that bench. My dress looks cool and summery in the picture, but underneath it lurked the terrible underwear Mother insisted on my wearing in those days. A child of any respectable family had to wear conventional clothes, complete with hat, even to play in the garden. This meant that under most of my dresses were layers and layers of stiff petticoats which hampered every movement I made.

The fact that children at that time always had to be well covered up was bad enough, but my mother also had a theory (which she probably heard decreed by a professor or some other expert on childrearing) that children had to wear woollen underwear next to the skin. You can't see, but I am wearing thick woollen stockings and 'combinations' which were a sort of long-sleeved tee-shirt and long-legged knickers all in one, made of scratchy cream-coloured woollen material. I had a woollen 'binder' on as well. This was a sort of band meant to fit snugly round my middle, but it would soon roll and twist in all directions. I remember the worst time, Sunday mornings, when my temper was frayed beyond endurance. My woollen underclothes, clean from the laundry, freshly-shrunk and tight, set off an irritation which drove me nearly crazy. Eventually – HALLELUIA! – my parents heard of something called Mr. Diamel's Hygienic Underwear which proved to be made of cotton with a vascular weave. Although the shape of Mr. Diamel's garments could be rather peculiar, the feel of them was infinitely better.

On my feet I had to wear boots, which were very much in vogue throughout my childhood, even for grown-up ladies. There were no such things as zips in those days, so the boots had to be laboriously buttoned up (usually with long-handled buttonhooks, to save bending down too far). Nanny always buttoned mine, and most ladies had to get their maids to do theirs because they were unable to bend at all owing to the tight whale-boned or steel-reinforced corsets they wore! We did not hear of bad backs much then: did these strait-laced affairs have some good effect on ladies' posture? Even so, I was glad I didn't have to wear a corset as a child. The ordinary underwear was bad enough.

Now is not the time to tell you about this, however. I must describe my family to you, because they will feature in this story almost as much as me.

At the time this photograph was taken I lived with my mother and father in London, in an unusual and interesting place called Bedford Park. The whole area, which was a mile or so north of the River Thames, had once been open countryside with lovely big old trees. In 1875 (about twenty-five years before I was born) a man called Jonathan Carr had an idea that he would build a sort of brand-new village there. The houses were specially designed to be attractive and artistic and Bedford Park was laid out so that no two houses looked quite the same. The streets, which had names like Addison Grove and Queen Anne's Gardens, were carefully fitted in around the lovely old trees.

My mother and me, with my brother Eric

I lived with my parents and my brother Eric (who was sixteen years older than me) in one of the houses in Bedford Park. Both of my grandmamas lived in Bedford Park, too, in separate houses. Papa's mother, who was called Caroline Boosey when she was a little girl, had become Caroline Blair Leighton when she married. She had moved to Bedford Park without her husband when the houses in it were nearly new. However, to explain to you why she moved there then, and why she was alone, I'll have to go back a bit further, before Papa was even born.

If you don't like family history, you can skip straight to Chapter Two here, but be warned – some of the people mentioned in this section appear later in the story. My family tree on page 130 may help you.

Papa's Scottish father, Charles Blair Leighton, who was my grandpapa, had eight younger brothers and sisters, which seems a large family now but was quite normal in those days. (The Blair Leightons did very well in the breeding line and a generation later when my father counted up his first cousins he found he had one hundred of them.) Charles and his brothers and sisters all lived with their parents Stephen Leighton and Helen Blair of Dunkeld. As a young man Charles decided to become a portrait painter, so after training at the Royal Academy Schools he began working in central London, hoping to establish himself where there were people wanting their portraits painted and plenty of opportunities for an artist to prosper. Two of his younger brothers, George Cargill Leighton and Stephen Leighton, also started working in London, but as printers and engravers, not painters. They called themselves Leighton Brothers and provided pictures for books and magazines including a very popular publication called *The Illustrated London News*. Later it became even more well-known for being the first magazine to have pictures in colour, and I remember the magazine from my childhood.

But we need to get back to my grandfather, Charles. Once he started to get some work painting portraits and was making enough money he was able to think about getting married. It was then he met Caroline, who had been brought up, just as he and his brothers had been, in the fierce Sandemanian religion based on the Scottish Kirk. Caroline was the daughter of a publisher called Mr. Thomas Boosey, who had a large house in Camden Hill Square. In 1849 she and Charles were married.

The story of my grandfather, Charles Blair Leighton, has a sad ending, however. Although he did obtain considerable recognition as a portrait painter and had several pictures hung in the National Portrait

Gallery and the Royal Academy, he died in 1855 aged only thirty-two. Poor Caroline, his widow, was left with two small children: Fanny, aged five, and Edmund, my father, aged two. She was also pregnant with a third child, so she was obliged to go back to live in her parents' home, where six months later the baby was born. It was a girl, who was given the name of Helen, although she was always known as Nellie. Once the baby was old enough and the two older children beyond the infant stage, Caroline determined to make an independent life for herself rather than having to live at home surrounded by her many brothers and sisters.

Being well educated, she eventually decided to start a boarding school for young ladies, and to do this she moved to a fresh part of London, the newly developed Bedford Park. She found a large house in a street called Blenheim Gardens, engaged German and French teachers as well as English ones and made a success of her venture. Her children, Fanny, Edmund and Nellie, grew up in the Bedford Park community, most members of which were involved in various arts such as music, painting, acting or writing, or in medicine.

Jonathan Carr, the founder of Bedford Park, had created an early form of Garden City, with its own local public house and even its own church designed by a famous architect called Norman Shaw. There was a thriving and well-equipped club in The Avenue, also designed by Shaw, with a theatre stage and rooms for social events, and it was here that my father, Edmund Blair Leighton, met my mother, Katherine Nash, for the first time.

Katherine was the eldest of four children. Like Papa, she also had a sister called Nellie. Nellie was two years younger than her and they had a brother William and, fifteen years younger still, another brother called Frank. Whereas my father's early life had been dominated by the Sandemanian religion, the Nash family came from a very different background. Katherine's mother, Sophia, was a fine pianist and friendly with some relations of the great composer, Felix Mendelssohn. In earlier years they had persuaded her to go and stay with them in Bonn, the town where they lived in Germany. She took her children with her and the Nashes later moved on to Paris. In Bonn, the children went to a local school where lessons were in German, and then later they attended the Sorbonne School in Paris, where they had to speak French. Because of this they had no choice but to become tri-lingual.

My grandmother Sophia parted from her husband in the end, and returned to England. Being devoted to any form of education, she too opened a private school in Bedford Park. Her daughter Katherine (my mother) was old enough by this time to be allowed to help as a teacher.

It had not been like this for Edmund when *his* mother, my other grandmother Caroline Blair Leighton, had set up *her* school for young ladies. He had not been allowed to help at all. In fact he had been discreetly sent off to a boarding school, where unfortunately he was desperately unhappy.

Have you ever read a book called *Nicholas Nickleby* by Charles Dickens? Nicholas Nickleby works in a school called Dotheboys Hall which is run by a cruel teacher called Wackford Squeers who beats and starves the children. Well, you can imagine what my Papa's school was like when I tell you that he later described it as a 'Squeers establishment'. Apparently the food was sparse and so horrid that on the rare occasions when he received some money from a relative he immediately bought a cream bun.

Edmund eventually left that terrible school and finished his education in a much nicer day-school in London called University College School. It was one of the first to abolish beating as a punishment, it had a gym to exercise in, which was very new in those days, and pupils had the chance to learn French and German there, as well as Latin. However, once

Edmund finished school altogether his life was a bit like Nicholas Nickleby's again. In Dickens' story, Nicholas is told by his uncle that he must work in order to make enough money to look after his widowed mother and his sisters. Well, Edmund, who had drawn and sketched all his life, longed to become a painter as his poor dead father Charles had been, but an uncle insisted that Edmund took a job in the City, in the tea market, I think, so he too could help support his widowed mother and his sisters. After a while, however, the family could see that Edmund still wished to become an artist, and he was told that he could be one, as long as he saved up enough money to look after himself during his first year as a painter. He agreed, and worked hard in the City to save as much as he could, but spent every spare moment on painting and drawing and attending night classes.

When he was nineteen he managed to gain entry into the Royal Academy Schools, where his father had once been a student. He hoped he would eventually get the chance to exhibit his work in the Royal Academy itself, as my grandpapa Charles had done. Having a painting accepted by the Academy for the yearly Summer Exhibition in the Great Room in Somerset House was very exciting for a young artist. It was described as having your work 'hung on the line' because of a wooden moulding running around the room at a height of about six feet from the floor. This was 'the line': bigger paintings were hung above it and smaller paintings below. My Papa had his first large painting 'hung on the line' when he was twenty-three, which is very young. Even the famous painter John Constable did not exhibit there until he was twenty-six. I still take pride in Papa's first success, although it happened in 1878, a long time before I was born.

Edmund went on working hard, doing illustrations for magazines like *Harper's Bazaar*, advertisements, fashion drawings and any other commercial work which came his way. However, it was only after several years of working long hours that, although not well off, he felt he was sufficiently established to get engaged. He and my mother, Katherine, both loved dancing and taking part in the many musical and dramatic activities at the Club in Bedford Park. Katherine also shared his interest in art, having studied painting at the Sorbonne School when her family lived in Paris. Being fond of each other and finding that they had much in common, they duly decided to marry.

Now, one of my father's uncles was Uncle John. He was the brother of my grandmother, Caroline Blair Leighton. In his youth poor Uncle John had been forced by their father, Mr. Boosey, to marry a particular girl, as the phrase went, "to make an honest woman of her". (This meant that a girl was pregnant and that the father of her baby ought to marry her.) However, it had turned out that Uncle John's wife had been neither honest nor pregnant and so their marriage was not a happy one, as you can imagine. John frequently visited his widowed sister Caroline and her family, and when he saw his young nephew Edmund and Katherine Nash together and realised how suited they were and how fond they were of each other he approved very much of their intended marriage. This was helpful, because of course Edmund did not have a father alive to guide him or advise his mother.

Interestingly, by the time my parents were married Caroline Blair Leighton had given up her school. However, she was anxious to keep occupied. Her brother John, who had been so helpful to Edmund, was working in the family business and had begun to publish music with some success. As well as printing music he produced a range of instruments including flutes. Flutes need special pads inserted in their keys, but the pads were hard to obtain at that time as they needed very accurate hand sewing. Caroline took on the task of sewing round the edges of small round pieces of kid, cut out by machine, inserting a smaller piece and then drawing it up into a pad and finishing it off. She did this so well that she continued the work for the rest of her life. In her old age she was looked after by my aunt Fanny, who was her oldest child and still unmarried. Fanny had always been interested in handicrafts and embroidery herself and, indeed, she had taught at the Acton and Chiswick Polytechnic, a college which was opened in the Bath Road in London, just on the fringe of the Bedford Park estate. Caroline's youngest child, Helen, tiny and very attractive and thus known by us as 'Little Aunt Nellie', had married and had three children.

My Granny, Caroline, with her oldest grown-up child (my Aunt Fanny)

Two

Living with a Painter Father

My parents' first home after they were married was one of the smaller Bedford Park houses, but after a few years they moved to 14 Priory Road where I was brought up and where Papa remained for the rest of his life.

Every painter has to have a studio to work in, and my father had his at home. It was really rather like a museum. One entire wall was hung with old musical instruments and others were laid out on a high shelf which ran round the room. I recall an arch-lute, a serpent, an Indian harp and banjos of every shape and national origin. My father had played the guitar in his youth and still had two very fine instruments.

The studio was entered from the oak-panelled hallway which had carved oak cupboards where steel helmets and other small pieces of armour were displayed. These had been collected for use in paintings of historical subjects. A heavy sound-proof door and then another at the foot of two steps led into a large ante-room with glass side-walls and roof, used for posing figures for 'out of door' scenes. From this a series of large folding doors opened into the studio, an ample room about thirty feet long by twenty feet wide. Although this was his working area where an entire

The corner of Papa's studio where the musical instruments and other painter's props were kept

scene might be built – maids were under strict orders never to touch anything – it was as well kept as a drawing room with its polished pine-strip flooring and Persian carpets.

I remember one funny incident with those carpets. I suppose I was about three at the time. After tea, at about five o'clock, I was allowed down to visit my father in his studio. In those days the streets outside were quagmires on wet days and there was one particular muddy place where people had to cross to gain entrance to The Common. An old man with a broom used to sweep a path through the mud and horse-droppings if you paid him a penny, and it was my proud privilege to hand it to him. Indoors in the studio my father was very amused one day to see me busy pretending to make a crossing on the polished floor between the rugs. I was using one of his set-squares as a broom, so he got another set-square

LIVING WITH A PAINTER FATHER

This is me out for a walk with Nanny, giving a penny to the poor crossing-sweeper

and joined in, saying things like "Oh, I'm getting a lot of mud here!" When I heard him say this I would immediately drop my set-square 'broom' and take over his.

He was very good at playing with me in the studio. There was an old chest there, and in it were lovely lengths of the fabulous silk fabrics Papa used for backgrounds in some of his paintings. When I was a little older, he would sometimes open the chest and play with me at shops - heaven for a small girl!

At the far end of the studio were three deep recesses beneath a balustraded balcony. In the central recess was the fireplace with

LIVING WITH A PAINTER FATHER

I have tried to paint Papa's studio here as I remember it

deep-silled windows on either side. One held a display of antique glass bottles, the other my mother's extensive collection of pewter. Sofas, hard and unyielding, stood against the side walls and above them were hung duelling pistols of every shape and kind with engraved silver butts. A half-sized billiard table was upended against a wall of the right-hand recess, from which a flight of stairs led to the gallery. In the left-hand recess, behind a tapestry curtain, lurked a life-size, jointed, bald-headed artist's model, with a pink stocking-covered body. Beyond this lay a well-stocked workshop with a bench and a huge cupboard. Another door led to a changing room for his models, complete with basin and separate lavatory, and beyond that you could go through a small greenhouse out into the garden.

*Papa had to pose specially for this photograph –
he wouldn't normally paint a picture already in its frame!*

Because Papa painted pictures set in earlier historical periods, he collected genuine costumes whenever possible and if none could be found accurate replicas would be made. For this a dressmaker would regularly come in daily for about two weeks at a time. A room on the top floor was taken over where she and my mother would make costumes based on fashion prints of the period or authentic contemporary drawings. They were undefeated and not only made beautiful dresses, carefully measured and fitted for the female models, but also entire male outfits. Some of the fabrics had elaborate patterns which my mother painted on with loving care.

Papa first sketched the costumes from his live models in some detail so that the garments could be transferred to the dummy, with the arrangement of the folds copied as nearly as possible. There they could be left in place until that part of the painting was completed. When more light was needed for a painting, a huge bookcase could be moved from a south window. This was done for the painting called *Prince Arthur Learning to Read*: for this work a complete mock-up of a stone-pillared window was also erected to enable the light and reflections to be represented as accurately as possible.

As well as the annual large work for the Academy, Papa produced many smaller paintings, some on canvas, others on wooden panels. Many of these would be studies but others were painted out of doors with the

*Some verses from a poem
I wrote for Christmas
about Papa's painting attire:*

My Father is a painter man
And loves his old clothes best,
He thinks there is no better plan
Than wearing them for rest.

To dressing he does not aspire,
Except on Christmas day,
And then his shirt front we admire-
In fact his whole array !

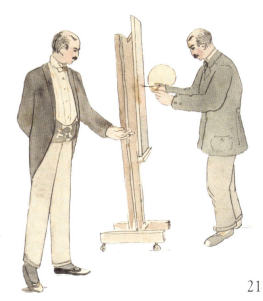

figures added in the studio. He was always impeccably dressed and while painting would just slip on a grey alpaca coat, which was loose and washable. He never spilled paint or made a mess. In fact, one model said that she could not believe Papa was an artist when she first saw him – he was too clean! My father laughed and replied that he had noticed that as artists got better, they got cleaner.

Papa always went for a walk before starting work and when he had finished work and carefully washed his brushes he walked again before the evening meal. He used to say that most of the artists who had been successful were those who had maintained strict mental discipline. However in his case this discipline was only imposed on himself and not upon his family and friends. He loved children and animals and always took a dog with him on his walks.

When out walking he was very observant and this, combined with his quest for suitable models, led to some embarrassing moments when his interest in certain handsome ladies was misunderstood. So great was his desire for female perfection that he would sometimes combine the face of one girl and the figure of another, thereby achieving a result that was perhaps too good to be true. I found that his informal portraits and sketches had far more real character.

Every year, before 'sending-in day' for the Royal Academy Exhibition at the beginning of April, Papa and many of the better-known painters in London had private shows of their work. Invitation cards were sent out for a certain date and during the afternoon of that day there would be a continuous stream of arrivals, mainly potential buyers and interested friends. The maids were kept busy ushering in the visitors and handing round tea, which was served in the dining room.

I suppose that in a way I was on show too, at an early age, although I was quite unconscious of the fact. As I grew older, I was expected to help

Visitors admired Papa's paintings at his Private Views - can you see me?

entertain and look after the visitors and take them through to the studio before they had their tea. (The entertaining and hostessing of large parties was a matter of course for children from my background, and although we may not always have liked it, it did stand us in good stead in later life.) Sometimes over a hundred and fifty people would call in one afternoon, so I was kept fully occupied. My cousin would also help, and we got considerable amusement from comparing notes about the comments visitors made. One which cropped up fairly often, usually expressed by someone who had little genuine interest in the paintings, was "What a beautiful frame!"

Not only was the main painting to be sent to the Academy on view, but perhaps as many as four or five other smaller works which could be sold directly from the studio. Other artist friends of Papa's also held Private Views in their studios and these were usually arranged amongst them on different dates so they could all visit each others' shows!

I liked going to see the other painters. One of them was a lifelong friend of my father's called Sir Frank Dicksee. We used to visit his large and curious house at Maida Vale which was run by his sister, Polly, a very shy, self-effacing lady. There had been an elder sister called Min, who had been my mother's closest friend, but she died some years before I was born. Min had been an artist, too – even more talented, some people said, than her brother.

Sir Frank and Polly both made a great fuss of me when I was a child, so I loved going to their house. We were shown a large glass cabinet in the drawing room, which could be wheeled outwards to reveal the entrance to a gallery and a staircase leading down to his studio. The whole place was rather solemn and mysterious, full of huge canvases each on its own easel. Part of Frank and Polly's house was occupied by an aged aunt called Miss Bernard, who was very fat, and who sometimes came to dinner at our house with them. I liked her, but she always reminded me of a hippopotamus, especially as she always wore clothes of a purplish-red, which added to the illusion.

LIVING WITH A PAINTER FATHER

Our friend Sir Frank Dicksee drew this picture of me when I was about four

More about our house

Three

More About Our House

I must return to the description of our own house in Bedford Park, however. I'm afraid to say that in winter our house was bitterly cold. There were gas fires upstairs (although they were of a rather primitive form) but in the downstairs rooms the only heat came from open fires. Coal was collected by the housemaids, in large boxes with handles, from an indoor cellar near the back door. The fire in the drawing room had to be lit by the parlourmaid, who then had to tend it and see that it stayed alight, even when there were members of the family in the room.

Because heating was almost entirely by coal and gas, and cooking was usually done on large coal-fired kitchen ranges (although there was the odd rather primitive gas cooker) most houses had several chimneys and they would all be belching out untreated smoke. Everything outdoors was covered in sticky black soot. The authorities tried to lessen the problem by building gasworks and factories with high chimneys but, as the old saying goes, 'what goes up must come down' and the smoke and sulphur fumes hung in the air, smelling foul and making it hard to breathe.

In an attempt to prevent dirt and fumes seeping into the house, my parents had frames fitted to the bedroom windows with a thin woollen fabric stretched over them to act as filters. After one day of evil-smelling fog, soot would cling to the cloth so that it looked like black velvet. This meant constant washing and, of course, there were no such things as washing machines. It all had to be done by hand or sent to one of the rare steam laundries.

The dining room, where I took the visitors to have their tea on Private View days, had heavy velvet curtains with both lining and interlining, presumably to try and combat the cold, but there were also tussore silk curtains directly against the windows, with real lace inserted at the edges. On the windowsills there were large oriental copper bowls holding plants called aspidistras, and the walls were covered in thickly-embossed Japanese wallpaper, coloured gold and deep sealing-wax red. There were also lots of pictures in heavy gold frames. The effect was rich and dignified, but it was almost completely dark in the back and corners of the room.

Then there was the hall which led to the studio, with its staircase going up to the bedrooms and bathroom on the first floor. We had a large bathroom with hot and cold running water and bathtime was a pleasure. When I was young Papa would often come up when I was in the bath and finish off his daily paintbrush-washing in the bathroom to be companionable. He would chat to me and ask me about what I had been doing during the day.

I have already mentioned some of the chores which were done for us by our maids. When I was a young girl, domestic life was very different from what it is now. I was often awakened in the morning by the sounds of activity as our maids bustled about their work. In those days all cleaning had to be done by dustpan and brush. To collect the dust, used tea-leaves were saved. When they were semi-dry they were sprinkled onto the carpets. The dry dust clung to the damp leaves and the whole mixture could be swept up together with a stiff brush.

Wooden floors were kept at a dangerously high state of polish with beeswax dissolved in turpentine, mixed up with a stick in 7lb jam jars. This was wiped on with one cloth and vigorously polished off with another. Sometimes maids were overzealous and polished beneath the corners of the Persian rugs, with surprising skating results for the unwary! The other woodwork in all the upstairs rooms and corridors in our house was protected by three coats of white gloss paint, kept in a state of perfect order by a fortnightly rub and polish with whitening, soft soap and water.

Our maids worked very hard to keep the house clean

I do not know if safety razors had been invented when I was young, but they were not in general use. Papa, my brother Eric and any other gentlemen staying in our house used 'cut-throat' razors, which required stropping. The strop was a leather strap which had a hand-hold at one end, and a ring at the other, which could be hooked onto any available knob. The ring was hooked, the leather was pulled taut with one hand and the razor's blade was stroked up and down the strop with the other. We all knew how far the gentlemen had progressed with their morning routine of washing, dressing and shaving when we heard the sound of stropping.

Stainless steel was not used for household knives very much at that time. They were of tempered steel instead, which had to be kept sharp by being rubbed regularly on a special board sprinkled with emery powder. Over the years the blades became worn down, shorter and shorter, into very strange shapes.

Although they worked hard, our maids rarely left unless they were about to get married, many remaining in the household for twelve or more years. Sometimes their places were taken by other members of their family. Our own staff usually included a cook, a parlourmaid and one housemaid, as well as 'Nanny', who looked after me when I was a small child. As I became more independent she was often asked to help the housemaid. In addition there was Anna, a German woman who came to clean the brass and scrub out the kitchen. We had a gardener, Mr. Poulton, who also cleaned the windows and an extra man came in once a month to polish Papa's collection of armour.

The maids wore stiffly starched white caps and aprons over pale blue or pink cotton frocks. Before serving lunch they would change into green alpaca dresses with fancy, lace-fringed aprons, caps, collars and cuffs, which were very becoming. These were their personal property and my mother generally gave them new ones at Christmas.

The parlourmaids took great pains with their appearance

The parlourmaids took great pains with their appearance and with ironing their aprons and caps. One used to make her own dresses out of fine cotton lawn with gathered frills round the edge. I used to love to watch her, after she had washed them, carefully finishing the edges with a special goffering iron which looked rather like several modern curling tongs joined together.

The parlourmaid was expected to help the housemaid make the beds and clean the bathrooms and so on while we had our breakfast. She would have set the table for this, made the coffee and put the eggs or kedgeree ready on a heated tray. In winter, my father's hot breakfast was placed on a kind of trivet in front of the fire in the studio.

The parlourmaid was kept pretty busy, as she was responsible for the pantry with all the glass and china and was also constantly keeping watch over the fires and answering bells (either the front doorbell or bells in the house summoning her for further instructions).

One of our parlourmaids, called Alice, always remained good-tempered and ready to enter into any joke, but her patience must have been tried at times, especially when my friends and I used to play with the speaking-tube which led from the first-floor down into the kitchen. We found it a source of great amusement and I used to call down it with pretend orders, but, amazingly, dear old Alice did not complain too much about this.

Of course, as well as the house to keep clean and tidy, meals to prepare and fires to keep going, there were clothes and bed linen to be washed, but the maids did not have to do much of this. In our household much of the laundry was collected and returned each week by the son of my grandmother's old washerwoman, who had married and set up a small and very efficient hand-laundry in Acton.

Four

My Parents Employ a Nanny

I NEED TO TELL YOU ABOUT Nanny now. Although I had a brother, Eric, who lived at home, he was so much older than me that I saw little of him and my life was much like that of an only child. In those days parents in well-off families did not see their children for most of the day, and living in Norman Shaw's Bedford Park, with its individually-designed houses, each with their own garden, and its artistically-minded community, my parents were surrounded by their own friends who often had comparable interests. It simply never occurred to them that a small girl also needed companions of her own age so, apart from a few carefully-chosen 'suitable' children who were sometimes invited to the nursery for tea, I rarely had anyone to play with.

My parents would pay me occasional visits and I would be taken downstairs for about half an hour after tea. I adored my mother, but she remained aloof and I had little response from her. It was my father who encouraged my imagination and entered into games of make-believe and later, when I was older, took me to the Wallace Collection and also to the Victoria and Albert Museum where we roamed around looking at the various types of period furniture. However, I spent most of my childhood in the nursery with Nanny as my constant companion.

My Parents Employ a Nanny

Nanny proudly pushing me in my perambulator

When I was born my parents had employed a professional nursemaid to look after me, and later Nanny had been engaged to take over from her. One of my early memories is of being about two years old and sitting in the large perambulator, well-wrapped in a white shawl of a honeycomb pattern with a comforting smell of wool. I was being pushed along by a squat, well-upholstered figure with a mountain of curly white hair, topped by an enormous black hat. That was Nanny.

She was about the same age as my mother (in her mid-forties) and was the widow of a soldier killed in the Boer War. Since his death she had spent her life as a nanny in various families. She was the oldest child of an enormous family although quite how many brothers and sisters she had I was never sure. She had left school at the age of ten to help her mother with the family brood, so it was not surprising that she was practically illiterate and had the greatest difficulty in reading even the simplest words. Personally very fastidious, with a pretty, fresh complexion, she remained somewhat childish in many ways. She was kind enough to me, but I have no memory of her playing with me until I was old enough to join her in simple games like Snap. In fact, I never really felt she had any warm affection for me.

Bathing was fun. Hairwashing was not!

Nanny would wash me and dress me when I was young, but she also had the task of washing my hair, which was something I did not enjoy. I had long thick hair and its regular washing was a penance I feared. Nanny's method was to pour a large can of water over my head, rub in Packer's Coal Tar soap and rinse by the same method. A great torrent of hot water, poured from above, entered my eyes and ears bringing the soap with it. The performance was excruciating.

My mother taught her to sew, and she would stitch away while I amused myself in the nursery. Occasionally I was allowed to have other children to tea with me, in preparation for which Nanny used to take me out to buy meringue fingers or delicious 'farthing buns', so called because they were four for a penny. In those days we had small coins called farthings and four farthings were worth one penny. There were twelve pennies in a shilling and twenty shillings in a pound, which meant that there were 240 pennies – or an amazing 960 farthings – in a pound. If you had spent £1 on farthing buns, therefore, you would have been able to get nearly a thousand buns for your money! You can see how even one pound was an enormous amount of money back then.

In another way Nanny nearly affected my eating habits for life. When I was about five, my mother discovered that there were many things I would refuse to eat. She decided that I should have lunch with her in the dining room, where she would offer me some of these things and see my reaction for herself. I cannot now recall what was put before me, but I know that whenever those particular dishes had appeared in the nursery for my lunch Nanny had always put me off trying them by saying "Oh, no, you wouldn't like that". I still felt I ought to refuse them when Mother offered them to me, but I vividly remember thinking how nice they looked, and a small voice inside me asking, "Should I give in?" Finally Mother positively ordered me to taste a small piece, however, and I ended up by finishing the lot! In a way this whole incident was strange, because in fact there was very little variation in our menu when we had no guests to eat with us. My mother liked to adhere rigidly to a diet of lamb cutlets followed by rice pudding and stewed apple, unless it was some special occasion.

When I was about six and a half I had to have a nasty operation for tubercular glands, and after this the doctor advised as much fresh air as possible. This suited Nanny perfectly, so every day after that I was taken out for a walk in the morning, another in the afternoon and then, after a short rest, out again. In wet weather I was weighed down by galoshes, which were heavy rubber shoes put on over your normal shoes. Nanny must have been a great walker, as my early years seem to have been one long trudge. My father believed in walking as the ideal means of keeping fit. The exercise certainly developed my calf muscles, and made the aching of them a torture, night after night.

Nanny knew another children's nurse who lived a few roads away, who looked after a girl a couple of months older than me and a boy in a pram about three years younger. My mother approved of the family, so we walked together for many years, but we children still had nothing in common after all that time, except that our nannies were friends.

The thing was, that Nanny always liked to talk to the other nurses and nannies she met while taking me out for walks. One nurse with whom Nanny struck up a friendship was looking after a little girl called Biddy Lutyens and her brother. They were the nephew and niece of a famous architect called Edwin Lutyens. The conversation between the two nannies was not meant for my ears and was sometimes rather colourful. Vivid descriptions of one of my Nanny's brothers being struck by lightning while under a tree and another being gored to death by a bull have remained with me during the rest of my life.

I remember being taken when very young beyond the outskirts of Bedford Park, some two streets beyond our own, where a lane ran between dykes edged with willows, which screened low-lying swampy meadows. I believe the meadows were below river level, which later made the sewage arrangements of that district very tricky. Later, when I was older, we would cross the footbridge over the railway line towards the rubbish dumps, some of which were of a considerable height. One year they were even covered in snow. I had a very smart toboggan and with this I had a wonderful time on their slopes with Biddy Lutyens and another girl called Ursula Tennyson, while Nanny watched patiently.

Still walking, on some occasions Nanny would take me through Acton to play in the fields round the prison of Wormwood Scrubs, which stood grim and alone. Then we would walk back though Gunnersbury Lane and Kew, arriving home very, very weary. Sometimes we went to the Gardens at Kew, and on those days I generally took with me pencil and paper and spent happy times taking down the names of plants which appealed to me. On my return home I proudly handed the list to Mother, who very often included them in her order to Carter Page, her usual horticultural supplier.

When I was a little older, I was sent fairly often with Nanny to Hampton Court. She was really very good, because History and Things Of Art meant nothing to her, and as she grew older her feet hurt quite frequently.

For years and years Nanny took me walking at least twice a day – sometimes three times!

My Parents Employ a Nanny

Poor Nanny! Possibly the only rest she got from the walking programme was when we went to the seaside. Once, when I was ten, Mother took her and me down to Margate, so that I could take the sea air and learn to swim. Even then, Nanny still suffered. We stayed at a boarding house and were able to go to an indoor, sea-water swimming pool, which was then quite unusual. I had a wonderful time because, apart from going to the swimming pool, I was also allowed to play on the sandy beach in the afternoons instead of being taken for walks. Here I made friends for the first time with a boy. His name was George, but I never fathomed his surname: it was something very Scottish. He said he enjoyed playing with me because I played more like a boy than a girl.

We children had a marvellous time, running over slippery rocks, looking into pools and outpacing Nanny, who took a dim view of it, suffering with her poor feet. George even gave me a present one day: he fumbled in his pockets, found a farthing, and treated me to some curious sweets which looked like small pebbles. All good things come to an end, however, and George had to return home before I did. I never met him again.

At the seaside we changed for swimming in bathing machines - strange wheeled huts which opened straight onto the water

Five

My Mother

When my brother Eric was born in 1886, Mother was looked after by the local doctor, but his attentions resulted in a long and deplorable series of miscarriages which left her a semi-invalid for fifteen years. In the end she consulted the pioneer women's doctor Elizabeth Garrett Anderson about her health and I am pleased to say that, after following Dr. Anderson's advice, Mother recovered. Soon afterwards, however, at the rather grand old age of forty-five, she found herself pregnant with me. I always say that it was my appearance in the world which put things right for her, but all the same Mother was rather embarrassed by her condition at that age. While she was expecting me she would only go out well-wrapped up in a voluminous cloak.

You may wonder how Mother spent her days if she was not looking after me. Well, running a house with several servants was always quite time-consuming: although the lady of the house did not cook, she had to plan the meals and tell the cook what to prepare, and although she did not clean the house and make the beds, she still had to organise the maids. She usually had to order the coal for the fires and the food for the kitchen as well. As the wife of a well-known artist Mother was also expected to receive his guests and be hospitable to them, and somewhere in all this she found time to socialise with her own friends as well.

In those days it was usual for a lady like my mother to have an 'Open Day', which was not really a whole day, but just a set time when she would always be at home for people to visit her. The day and time were carefully chosen so as not to coincide with the Open Days of her friends. If you were invited to an Open Day you would receive a a small card, about four inches by two, at the bottom of which were printed the words:

> *Mrs. So-And-So*
> (whatever the lady's name was)
> *will be delighted to receive*
> *at 4 p.m. on every third Thursday*
> (or whatever the chosen day might be).

In those days ladies could not easily telephone their friends to invite them to the house: we did not have a telephone and neither did most other people we knew. If one was urgently needed, we had to go to the local Club, but there the instrument was stationed between the inner and outer entrance doors, which made hearing difficult and privacy almost impossible.

When the visitors started arriving for the Open Day, it was the duty of the parlourmaid to answer the doorbell and show them in, preceding them to the door of the drawing room and formally announcing them by name. Uninvited callers or people considered unsuitable would be told at the front door, "Madam is not at home!"

On these occasions, when the parlourmaid served the tea she would bring in a tea caddy, either of silver or of wood, and a silver kettle on a hinged stand. This held a methylated-spirit burner so that the hostess could make tea herself at her convenience. There would generally be a plate of dainty sandwiches, a large cake, and some smaller ones carried around on a special little piece of equipment. This consisted of three or four small trays set in a hinged frame which folded flat when not in use. A handle on the top enabled it to be politely carried round by a helpfully-inclined visitor, who might on many occasions be the curate of the local church. For this reason the device was known as 'The Curate's Delight'.

"Tell them we're not at home!"

The entertaining and hosting of large evening parties was another of my mother's duties. It was a part of my childhood I remember well, because Nanny would send me down to the drawing room (I suppose, to be displayed to the guests) before the adults went in to a formal supper party. When the parlourmaid came to announce that dinner was served, all the guests arranged themselves in order of precedence, the men offering their arms to their dinner partners, and then they all proceeded through the panelled hall to the dinner room.

My parents' dinner guests processed in pairs to the dining room

I then had to go back upstairs to bed. I always slept with Nanny in what was called the night nursery, and even when I had almost reached my full adult height I still slept in the cot I had used as a tiny child. My mother could not bear to feel that I had outgrown my little bed (I regret to say that she and Papa did not stop calling me 'Baby' until I was about six years old) so she had a short piece of mattress specially made to extend it. The end of the metal cot was filed off, and this extra piece of mattress was supported on a chest at the foot of the bed. Although, when covered by a sheet, the bed then looked long enough for me, in fact the piece of mattress on the chest was still unattached, so my feet tended to slip into the hollow between the two bits of mattress. This was very tiresome, and the only way to remedy it was to remake the bed with the short piece of mattress at the head, so that the longer mattress would bridge the gap between bed and chest. I had to do this practically every day, for although I frequently demurred, Nanny would insist on making my bed the wrong way. I suppose it was less trouble to her to do it that way.

Mother certainly occupied herself a great deal in thinking about my upbringing and organising it. Although she and Papa were not prepared to spend much of their time in my company, they were most concerned about my welfare and avidly followed various theories on the subject. Most of these caused me considerable discomfort and I have to confess that I did all I could to resist their imposition.

In 1904 a man called Lieutenant J. P. Müller had published a book of exercises called *My System – 15 Minutes' Exercise a Day for Health's Sake*. Among his recommendations were regular exercise and clean living, eight hours' sleep a night and the avoidance of stress and over-eating. The exercises themselves, known by us as 'Mr. Muller's', were aimed to tone as many muscles in the body as possible.

My father, who was keen on keeping fit and did early morning exercises himself, persuaded my mother to take up these strange antics with me, so I had to perform them with her before breakfast every day in front of an open window to benefit from the fresh air. This continued for some years, I'm afraid to say.

The next development was far more to my taste. My father had a horizontal bar erected between the walls in the passage outside the nursery and said, "Now, my girl, every time you go along the passage, pull yourself up to your chin!" My brother Eric demonstrated how to do this, and even went one better, raising his extended legs and swinging himself over the top. I never achieved that, but after a while I did find that I could get my chin up to the bar. A second bar was put up in the garden but was less popular as the soot-laden air made it sticky and unpleasant. In fact, if friends came to tea we used to convert the nursey passage into a sort of indoor play park. We rigged up a swing from the bar and had great games. We also created a most enjoyable slide by removing the long rugs and using the polished floor, but this was rather hard on our clothing, especially our underwear, so my guests and I used to tuck our dresses up into some old knickers kept expressly for this purpose.

We did Mr. Muller's exercises every morning for many years

Six

How I was Educated (or not)

YOU MAY WONDER how I had any friends if I never went to school. Well, from about the age of five I did go to a dancing class held at a local school, so I knew other children who went there. In talking to them I discovered that they were all learning to read and write, and by the time I was about eight I felt I must have some lessons. I had been drawing since memory began, of course, but had no idea how to form letters, so I asked my mother to teach me to write.

One exciting day she produced a copy book, sat me up at the nursery table and showed me how to make 'pot-hooks'. These were what people called the sort of squiggles which helped children to begin writing. They were rather like the loops which go downwards from the letters 'y' and 'g' but handwriting in those days was very squiggly, as many more letters of the alphabet had these loops. They did look a little like the hooks in the kitchen where Cook hung up the pots. I think that my mother found this pot-hook copying rather boring (I certainly did!) so she left me to get on with it, and this performance went on at intervals for the next couple of years, although only when we were in London, never when we were holidaying in the country.

Apparently some old professor who wrote and talked about the upbringing of children (possibly the same idiot who had insisted on children wearing woollen underwear next to the skin!) had told my parents that in his opinion no child should be taught lessons before the age of eight. My parents went one better and it was not until one day when I was ten that I was finally told that I was to have a governess, and that I was to go down to the drawing room to meet her. I was thrilled, and left the nursery to go downstairs walking on air.

On opening the drawing room door I found my mother talking to a veiled and hatted lady sitting with her back to the window, but I could not see the lady's face. I went up to my new governess in joy only to find, to my utter horror and disappointment, that it was just my nineteen year-old cousin, dressed up for the occasion. It had been decided that she should teach me, although she was very young and had no experience of teaching at all.

She was one of Little Aunt Nellie's three children, a sweet, kind girl and she really did her best to teach me, but – bless her heart! – she was sadly short of grey matter. Years later I learned from her that she had never managed to read a book through to the end in her life. However, she bravely soldiered on with our 'lessons' and I learnt to read, write and say my tables. Mother provided the books and drew up a timetable. History consisted of learning the dates of kings and queens of England. When I knew those, I had to learn the dates of various battles, with no idea where any of them had taken place or what they were about! A modern child would have gone on strike in the first week, but this curious arrangement lasted until I was about twelve, when at last I was allowed to go to the nearby 'dame school' where I had always been taken for my dance classes. Even then I only went to school in the mornings: the afternoons had to be kept clear for – yes, you guessed it – long walks with Nanny.

How I was Educated (or not)

A dame school was not a proper Government-run school, but just a little school which an old lady might set up, usually in her own house, to teach a few local children. Their parents paid her but she could rarely afford to employ another teacher, so she might teach more than one class in the same room. My school was run by a lady called Miss Dolman, who was the sister of a well-known artist. She was a clever and dear old thing, but very hampered by poverty and by the necessity to care for a slightly mentally-retarded sister, whom we knew as Miss Kate. Miss Kate would occasionally emerge from the nether regions of the house wrapped in a scarlet crocheted shawl, only to be hastily sent packing by her sister.

In the earlier days when I had been to dancing classes, there had always been a neat elderly maid to open the door and the place was fairly spick and span, but at the time when I actually began school, no servants were visible and I think the head, Miss Dolman, who did the bulk of the teaching, had to be the cleaner (if indeed any cleaning *were* done), the cook, the fire-stoker and general dogsbody as well. She also had to be a warder to her progressively more and more annoying sister. Poor old soul!

When I began at the school I was put in a lower class with children about two years younger than me, but I soon got fed up with this and asked Miss Dolman if I could sit with my friends in the higher class. She told me that I was in the lower class because she had been asked by my parents "not to press me in any way" or, in other words, to make sure that the lessons I learned were not remotely challenging. I was furious when I heard this, so I borrowed my friends' books and found out about their work for the following day. When I got home I pored over the books until I was completely word-perfect and then the next day marched up to Miss Dolman and informed her I was going to sit in the higher class from then on. She asked me how I could, when I did not know as much as them, but when school started and I sat with my friends she found that I did indeed know enough, so she said, "Well, I can't stop you from being here now", and that was that.

There was a girl called Ursula Tennyson whom I liked the best in the school and when, later, she and I became the oldest pupils we were allowed a small upstairs room in which to do our work. It was thick with dust, however, and this was more than I could stand, so I packed a small briefcase at home with a duster and cleaning things and Ursula and I cleaned the room every morning before lessons. Miss Dolman was only too thankful.

Arithmetic was taught by a rather frightening visiting mistress called Miss Ratty, who lived up to her name, but I missed out on arithmetic altogether because Miss Ratty only came on two afternoons in the week and on Saturday mornings. In the afternoons I was not at school, of course (walking with Nanny!) and on Saturday mornings I now had my dancing class at the South Kensington Dance Academy. There I was taught by a woman called Miss Phipps.

I enjoyed the dance lessons, but one day Miss Phipps told my mother that my back was not as straight as it should be and that I needed massage. Consequently I was taken to a house in Harrington Gardens, South Kensington, which had a gym. There I was taken into a small room, undressed and pummelled all over with foul-smelling oil by a masseuse who turned out to be Miss Phipps' aunt. This continued for some weeks, after which Miss Phipps came to our house and proceeded to pummel and oil me herself. One day when my mother was out of the room, she pushed up one of my legs and held it there, claiming, on Mother's return, that one of my legs was shorter than the other. I protested, but no-one took any notice of what I said. I fancy that Miss Phipps was quite well paid!

My mother had an extraordinary facility for ignoring anything she did not want to know about and made some weird choices of people to come and teach me extra subjects. When I was a little older a comic and rather unpleasant elderly French teacher from Miss Dolman's Dame School, whom we had to call *Madame*, came to tea once a week to hold French conversation sessions with Biddy Lutyens, Ursula Tennyson and me. Madame smelled. I fancy it was beer, and I am afraid I got up to every prank I could think of. I would hide so that she could not find me and once I put some planks and dust sheets across the stairs with a notice saying "Please use the back stairs" (an impossible instruction, as we had no back stairs in that house!) To give the old thing her due, she really took it very well and at least it used to shorten the ordeal. I did learn as much French as I could, however, if only because my mother would talk to my father in French about anything I was not meant to hear. My

Biddy, Ursula and I drank tea with Madame, and learned to speak French

I protested against my elocution lessons from the top of the piano

father was not a natural linguist and before long I was able to understand her before he could.

Another horror produced in the name of education was an elocution mistress. I cannot believe she had any real qualifications, but she had taught at a school which my cousin attended. She had horrid spots all over her face and I am sure her hair had never seen water. I had to learn futile, arch little poems which she tried to make me illustrate with ridiculous, artificial gestures. After a few weeks I decided something must be done about it, so I climbed onto the top of the upright piano and refused to budge. That did it. She told my mother that I was so naughty she could not continue to teach me. My mother agreed, but not without a twinkle in her eye.

Although my parents had left my schooling rather late, I was eventually able to read very well and this was partly because of an interesting promise my father made me one birthday. I was given a bureau with a bookcase above it and when it was installed in the nursery Papa (who loved literature himself) came in with an edition of *David Copperfield*, placed it on the shelf and told me he would give me another book as soon as I had finished reading that one. He explained that in this way I would be able to fill my new bookshelf with classic literature: every time I finished one work, he would buy me another.

At first I found this hard going, but it soon became an expensive promise for my father to keep. With great enjoyment I ploughed my way through all the works of Charles Dickens, Sir Walter Scott, Mrs. Gaskell and George Eliot.

Seven

Outside the House in London

In Bedford Park, as elsewhere in London in those days, there were many street sounds which are now no longer heard (and, indeed, sights which are no longer seen).

Firstly, of course, was the sight and sound of horses in the street. Most tradesmen – that is, shopkeepers or their employees – would come on foot to the back door to deliver or take orders once or even twice a day, but milk was delivered daily on a special float drawn by a patient horse. When it stopped the milkman always shouted "MILKO!" to announce his wares. Housewives or domestics would issue from the houses with jugs and he would ladle milk into

Maids came out of the houses to collect milk from the milkcart

the jugs from a large brass churn on the float. The horse would then quietly move onto the next house without being told.

Sometimes the clip-clop of horses was followed by a scrubbing sound which echoed outside Papa's studio; looking out, we saw a diminutive man with a dustpan and brush retrieving the horse-droppings for the benefit of his garden. I never discovered where he lived, but my father said that he was a well-known comic music hall artist, known as Little Titch.

I once saw the entire road covered in straw to a depth of about

Little Titch would sweep up horse-droppings for his garden

eight inches. I was very mystified by this until I was told that someone was ill, and that the straw was used to deaden the sound of horse-drawn traffic with its iron-covered wheels and iron-shod hooves.

On the main roads, with all the horse traffic, the surface became very messy. There were certain crossing places with a raised surface so they could be cleared for pedestrians (particularly necessary at a time when the fashion was for skirts which virtually swept the floor) and these main crossings were each manned by a sweeper, who expected a penny for his work. As I mentioned before, I was usually permitted to put the penny into his outstretched hand.

When horse-drawn buses were being phased out, my father said I should be taken on the top of one so I would remember what they were like. They were double-deckers with an external stair at the back. There was no roof, so if it was raining a sort of waterproof cover was provided to protect the passengers. This looked a bit like a doormat with oilcloth on the outer side and a harsh flannel lining. It was held in place by eyelets which fitted over two brass pegs, one on the side of the bus and another on the seat. The seats had backs and were made of horizontal slats of varnished timber.

*Nanny and I travelled well-covered up,
on the top deck of a horse-drawn bus*

In the streets we often saw and heard people selling things. The man who sold muffins walked along clanging a large bell, selling his wares from a big wooden tray covered in green baize which he carried on his head. I never tasted one of his muffins but I believe that he had a lively trade. One man went the rounds with baked potatoes and another with hot chestnuts, and the sound of the girl who sang "Oh, who will buy my sweet lavender?" could not be resisted.

The lavender-seller would sing her irresistible song

I loved the organ-grinder and his tiny monkey

The visits of the hurdy-gurdy man were great fun. His tiny monkey, in a bright red coat, held out a hat for pennies while his master turned the handle of his music box. I was also very interested in the sight of an enormous brown bear with a collar and chain, walking on his hind legs beside a man who was waving a collecting box.

Something you don't see in the street nowadays is the twinkle of metal hairpins scattered over the pavement. It was the fashion during my childhood for ladies to pile masses of hair on the top of their heads or in a chignon (a twisted bun) at the base of the neck, and of course many pins were required to keep these styles in place. The hairpins, which escaped in large numbers from the coiffures of passing women, were mainly bronze or black and about four inches long. It was good fun on a walk to keep a tally and see who could spot the greatest number: the best hunting-grounds were the small square beds of a tree-lined pavement.

At dusk, the lamplighter carried round his pole on which he kept a hooded flame. He would push it up through a hole in the lamp, automatically turning on the gas and lighting it in one movement. The roads were quite well-lit at crossroads, but not so well elsewhere. I do not recall being conscious of the smell of gas, but might well not have noticed it because our houses, too, were all lit by gas.

I would try to get Nanny to stop and let us watch the dancing bear

Eight

My Childhood Companions – Dolls and Dogs

Although no-one actually entered into my games when I was little, dolls were my solace and I had quite a collection. My mother, who as I have said was an expert needlewoman, enjoyed making them exquisite clothes and I was content to dress and undress them as gently as if they were living children. Indeed they needed careful handling as their heads were made of porcelain and they were very fragile. Some of the most attractive were made in Germany, their faces modelled from real children. They had genuine hair which could stand constant brushing.

On one occasion, I inadvertently let go of the doll's pram and the boy doll suffered a smashed head, the horror of which is still vivid in my memory. Although my mother managed to find a replacement of the same model, my maternal eye could detect the very, very subtle difference and I couldn't feel the same way about the substitute. I never quite accepted him.

I even made dolls out of other inanimate things. When Nanny took me out for walks and talked to other nurses she met, she often mentioned her brothers and sisters-in-law. For me, this sounded like fun, and her stories triggered a game of make-believe in which my miniature croquet set became a family. As I steered the balls around with my mallet they assumed various roles and the different colours took on a range of personalities. The blue ball always behaved well, but the red one was a sore trial.

While I was tiny we still had an ancient fox terrier called Jo who had been a treasured pet in the family for many years before I appeared. She would suffer no advances from me, but if I were ever unwell she would jump up onto the foot of my bed to guard me and sit there firmly, always with her back to me. She guarded her master's property well and on the occasions in winter when Papa's breakfast was served in the studio she never sampled it, however appetising the smell, for her integrity was complete. Not so Mr. Tomkins, the cat, who had no such foolish ideas of honesty! He would steal whatever he could, and there was a fine hullabaloo if Jo caught him at it.

I do not know exactly how long these two survived, because for various reasons I did not often see them. Jo did not deign to enter the nursery regions if she could help it and I kept well out of the way of Mr. Tomkins after once receiving a nasty scratch from him.

After Jo's death I remember a series of dogs. One came to an unrevealed end and another was dispensed with when it was discovered that his rather unexpected activities could not be controlled. His name was Tim and he was an attractive, lively little terrier; friendly, but bent on investigation and adventure. He survived eating the contents of my watercolour paintbox (which contained poisonous blue paint!) and also leaping off a first floor balcony.

My Childhood Companions – Dolls and Dogs

My father was very fond of animals and when I was ten, I was taken to the Battersea Dogs Home to choose a dog of my very own. A thin and very frightened wire-haired terrier bitch, which had been found lost and starving in some back street, was brought out. The staff at the Dogs Home thought she might have been abandoned when she reached the age where she needed a dog licence.

I was entranced. When we got home my brother said she reminded him of little Emily in *David Copperfield*, so Little Emily (or 'Little Em') she became, and she and I had ten years of mutual devotion. At first she fled at the sight of any male; it was obvious she connected them with past

Little Em loved being dressed up and wheeled in the doll's pram

bad treatment, but after a while she also became devoted to my father. I had still played with dolls when I was on my own, but now Little Em replaced them. She would let me dress her in their clothes and would even stay in the doll's pram, lying flat on her back with a lace bonnet tied under her chin. Nothing mattered so long as she was loved and MADE A FUSS OF – in fact, one day I could not find her anywhere, and at last discovered her waiting in the pram. When our family went to Norfolk on holiday each year we took her with us, and in the country she loved going in the governess cart and was often found sitting in it hoping for a ride.

One year when we were in the country I was horrified to find that my little dog Em appeared to be very ill. She kept slumping down, hardly conscious, and was evidently in great distress. I showed her to Mother, who said at once that she must have eaten something that disagreed with her, and that the remedy was castor oil. This she deftly administered, but after about half an hour a large lump appeared above the poor animal's eye. The 'illness' had been a bee sting, which soon ceased to trouble her, although I don't know how long she suffered the effects of the castor oil!

Me training little Em

My brother had his own dog for a while, too. One day a disreputable-looking gipsy accompanied by a few unappetising followers arrived at the Norfolk house leading a large rust-coloured lurcher on a piece of rope. My brother immediately fell in love with the brute when the gipsy told him it could outpace a hare in flight and demonstrated that it could clear a five-bar gate with effortless ease.

Eric persuaded my parents to let him purchase the dog, and I remember the gipsy's parting words. "Hey!" said the man, "'E won't let a policeman come near the place. Nay, you don't have to pay for him on the train, either, 'e slips that quick under the seat."

This was proved true on our return journey to London, when the dog dived under the seat as soon as we set foot in the railway carriage and lay doggo until our arrival at Liverpool Street.

Care had to be taken to avoid going near the lurcher when he was feeding, but it became my job to take him out on our interminable walks where, having an affinity to animals, I found I could quite easily control him.

The end came when one day my mother was giving him a much-needed bath. He suddenly turned on her and went for her face. Her reflexes were of marvellous speed: she wrapped the waiting bath-towel round his head and, as he leapt out of the bathtub, caught him a mighty wallop on his backside, which sent him careering out of the door. Luckily, my mother got away with no more than a nasty bruise on her forehead from his teeth, but that was the end of the gipsy dog's stay in our household.

My Childhood Companions – Dolls and Dogs

You can see the gipsy dog with Mother, Eric and me in this photo

Nine

JACK THE DONKEY

WHEN WE WERE IN NORFOLK we often needed to get from place to place or go to the shops in Bungay, three and a half miles away from where we were staying, so my family bought a governess cart to be pulled by a donkey. It was a noisy vehicle with iron-shod wheels but looked fine with its locally-made harness of gleaming leather and brass fittings. The most important aspect of it to me, however, was

Our donkey Jack could pull the governess cart with Mother, my friend Greta and me in it

the young donkey acquired to pull it. His name was Jack. He was the gentlest, most patient creature imaginable, but he also had a strong sense of mischief and a will of his own. He became my greatest friend and confidant and never seemed to mind being hugged or how much I talked to him.

When I was very small my father, who loved country walks, thought it would be a good idea for me to ride on the donkey's back, so I could be taken through the narrow deeply-rutted lanes and woodland paths which were quite impassable with a pram. A special saddle was made, like a small leather armchair, so that I could sit sideways on Jack's back, but unfortunately it was a complete failure. Old Jack was much too clued-up to suffer the indignity of such a silly piece of apparatus. He simply

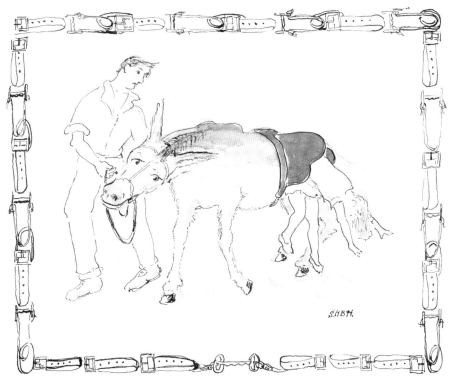

Trying to ride on Jack's back was never a great success

took an enormous breath and held it till I was firmly strapped on – and then let it out. The result was that the girth was now far too loose and so I slowly slipped round, still in the chair, until I was hanging upside-down under his tummy.

For me, life in the countryside was lots of fun. Not only my much-loved dog Em, but Jack and a pony called Kitty, which we added to our ménage a few years later, were my constant companions. I used to lead the three of them round the nearby fields holding a piece of string I had tied round the pony's neck and with literally just a cotton thread round that of Jack the donkey, who would often let the dog sit perched on his back.

Me with my trained animals, Kitty, Jack, and Little Em

If I found Jack lying on his side, I would sit beside him and he would lay his head on my lap and wobble his soft, mobile lips. He could accept any amount of attention but if I tried to ride him, oh, no! He would lower his head, raise his back and gently slide me down over his ears.

How I loved Jack! And I think he loved me, too

Because the heavy mowing machine and the water-filled roller for the tennis court were hard for the gardener to pull, it was decided that Jack should help. To prevent his sharp hooves from ruining the lawn, two pairs of neat leather boots were made for him by a harness-maker in Bungay. He did not seem to object to these, and once he was fitted with traces he meekly pulled the machines once a week. The gardener only had to steer, so Jack did all the work, but at least he was the centre of attention.

On journeys he was somewhat prone to spells of lameness. These were always on the outward trip, which he sometimes made on three legs (as if his other leg were too lame to use), but curiously, he would have recovered for the homeward journey, which was taken at a spanking trot. Sometimes on the outward journey he tried to turn back towards home long before we had reached our destination and had to be 're-orientated'. Poor Jack! A smart rap on the crupper had to be administered to make him proceed, albeit grudgingly, in the direction we wanted.

Jack was also 'allergic' to paper and flatly refused to pass any scrap lying in the road. Mother would have to hand down a penny to any village boy standing at the roadside and ask him to remove the offence from the donkey's path before Jack would move on. Jack did not like to get his feet wet, either, so he was apt to take a hop over puddles, making travelling in the governess cart quite precarious.

Kitty was looking for Jack, but he had cunningly hidden from her

When Kitty the pony arrived, she and Jack became great friends, but Kitty was rather bossy and old Jack could not take that for long. One day my father witnessed the curious sight of Jack hiding from her. Papa was chopping wood outside a farm building, when to his surprise the door behind him creaked and he turned to see it gradually opening. Jack, who had been inside the building, came to stand in the doorway and stayed there some time watching my father at work.

Presently there was the sound of hooves approaching. Jack pricked up his ears and as Kitty trotted round the corner he backed into the shed, firmly pushing the door shut from the inside. Kitty looked all around, but seeing no sign of Jack she went away, whereupon Jack pulled the door open again and peeped out to see if the coast was clear!

One morning I could not find Jack for love or money. I searched the stables, I searched the fields and the garden but there was no sign of him anywhere. Dejected and very worried, I returned to the house for assistance. As I entered the large stone-flagged kitchen, who should I see but Jack walking round the table with a very long freshly-baked loaf called a 'quartern loaf' (about twice as big as modern loaves) sticking out of the front of his mouth like a large cigar. The bread, having just been delivered by the baker, was very fresh. Soaking up Jack's saliva,

Greedy Jack got a nasty surprise when he tried to steal the bread

it expanded every time he opened his jaws, and he was getting very worried because he could not either eat it or get rid of it.

This was not the first time he had been indoors, however. His manners were so perfect that I would sometimes lead him through the house if I wanted to talk to my parents. He never upset anything but my mother took a dim view of his excursions into the drawing room.

Jack could open the latch of any door or gate and it was a continual game to stop him from going into the garden and feeding off my mother's favourite roses. He was also adept at letting Kitty in, too. Then all hell would break loose, as nothing pleased them more than to play hide and seek with us. They would let us get fairly close and then gallop off at full tilt along the paths and round the trees in the orchard and, worse still, over the tennis lawn, cutting huge furrows as they skidded to a halt.

Sometimes Jack escaped into the outside world by opening gates and then it took us even longer to find him. Opposite the school in the village was a railed-off portion of field which served as the village pound. Stray animals were put there for security until claimed by their owners. Jack was found there on occasions, but the worst consequence of his penchant for opening gates happened once when neither he nor Kitty could be found for a whole day. They were eventually discovered on the local squire's lawn, where they were definitely not appreciated.

Because of this escapade, my father decided to put a new fastening on the gate to our drive. Jack watched while Papa fitted it, but no sooner had my father picked up his tools to depart than Jack walked slowly up and opened the gate in a marked manner, looking very pleased with himself. My father muttered under his breath and set about boxing in the fastening completely. Jack waited patiently while this was done and then slowly went up to the gate again and in a few seconds had it open. After some considerable thought my father fixed a hook on the far side of the

JACK THE DONKEY

gate. This finally foxed Jack – but also baffled visitors, who often could not open the gate either.

One day the pony was being groomed in the stable, which had a high sill at the entrance. My mother was standing on this sill while giving directions about something or other. Jack, who was always rather jealous

Jack could be very naughty at times

of attention being given to the pony, came silently up behind my mother, lowered his head, pushed his nose firmly between her legs and then lifted his head violently. Mother soared spread-eagled through the air, and was caught in the arms of Tom, the horrified and astonished gardener's boy. I was convulsed with mirth. Luckily Mother always saw the funny side of things, but from then on if she heard Jack approaching from the rear she invariably took avoiding action.

During the winter, when we had returned to London, Jack and Kitty were separated. Kitty stayed down in the village with a man called Pumfrey, who had been our gardener and groom but was by then the local publican, while Jack went to a local farmer, who found him useful for short journeys. When we returned in the summer it was clear where those journeys had taken him, as Jack would stop firmly at every pub and took a great deal of persuading to move on.

Young Pumfrey always looked after Kitty in Norfolk while we were in London

Ten

Winter in London, Summer in Norfolk

At home in London in the winter, I had fun playing with my dolls and pets, visiting Papa in his studio and, once I started attending dancing classes, going to visit the friends I had made or inviting them to the nursery for tea. Later, of course, I went to school as well. Added to that there was always the excitement of Christmas. Every year at Christmas there was a big family party which included all my father's family and my mother's younger brother and his wife. Mother was always very busy with the table decorations; I remember an accordion-pleated silk table-centre in the folds of which were swathes of delicate foliage and huge crackers.

After the standard Christmas dinner, we all went into the studio where every year there would be a grand surprise. One year it was a huge Christmas tree surrounded by piles of prettily wrapped presents. Once, when I was about five, I was allowed to stay up and hand out the gifts, dressed as a white fairy. I wore a tarlatan tutu sprinkled with large silver embroidered stars and proudly waved a silver wand with an even bigger star on the top. Another year, a huge imitation Christmas pudding was contrived, made out of a series of wooden hoops covered in material or paper and painted to look like the real thing. It was placed on a large central table and when it was served the top was removed and – lo and behold! – out I popped and handed round the presents which had been hidden inside. Family presents at Christmas were not on the small side. My parents were extraordinarily generous to their less well-off relations. One year, I remember, a large dining room carpet was lugged out for Little Aunt Nellie, as her own carpet had become threadbare.

The excitement of Christmas began long before the event. I had sixpence a week pocket money, of which fourpence was always deposited in the Post Office Savings Bank while the rest was put aside for the careful purchase of gifts. There were never-to-be-forgotten times when I was allowed to go to the Penny Bazaar, which had a wonderful assortment of fascinating things to buy, including toy theatres where the scenes were changed by turning rollers. Also sold at the bazaar were lots of household goods interesting to grown-ups, which made affordable presents.

At home in London during the autumn, winter and spring, my father, who was quite well-known as a painter, was very busy. He painted large studio works for the Royal Academy Summer Exhibitions as well as smaller paintings which had a ready sale. For these he needed good natural backgrounds which were authentic, and he was always interested in painting and sketching old buildings. He needed rest, too, after the completion of the big Academy pictures, so he and Mother would rent old farmhouses and manor houses during the summer months in various parts of the country, where they could invite their friends to stay, as well as cousins of Eric's vintage so that my brother would have other children to be with. While he was in the country Papa made sketches, studies and small landscapes which were delightful in themselves. These could then be used to provide backgrounds for his numerous pictures of figures in period costume.

Travelling to fresh locations each year became difficult once he and Mother were encumbered with me as a baby, my nurse, my cot and all my other attendant paraphernalia, so they decided to find a place to rent on a regular basis. In those days, rents were very cheap, and if people took a property for any length of time they could make alterations and repairs to the buildings, cultivate the garden as they wished and generally treat the place as if it were their own.

My parents had once spent a pleasant summer in a small manor house in Norfolk, at Ellingham, where they had made some friends and Eric had found young people of his own age. While they were there, they heard of a charming old farmhouse called Kirby Green, on the estate of the moated Kirby Manor. Owned by the local squire (who also owned and farmed the many surrounding acres) it was in the more remote and hilly part of his land, two and a half miles from the nearest village of Kirby Cane. My parents hired a horse and trap and went to see it. Although a great deal needed to be done to it, they fell in love with the place and took it on a yearly lease. This arrangement lasted for eighteen years. From then on we would migrate to Norfolk, complete with our London household staff, for about three months each summer and

Here is a photo of the front of our Norfolk house

sometimes also for three or four weeks at Easter. Despite our interesting life in London, my happiest memories are of our days spent in Norfolk during the summer.

About a week before we set off, a notice with the initials 'C P' in red letters on green card was put in the hall window. Men from the removals firm Carter Patterson would duly turn up with a large horse-drawn lorry in which they collected all our trunks and packages and arranged for their safe delivery. One year when we set off for the summer there seemed to be even more luggage than usual, amounting to twenty-one large items. I remember one item was the child's bath (known as a saucer-bath) in which I was always bathed while in Norfolk. This was made of metal, brown on the outside and white on the inside, which, as it had a lid and could be locked, doubled as a useful piece of luggage, holding toys and so on.

To get to Norfolk ourselves we had to go to Liverpool Street station with all our hand-luggage and catch a train. When I was very young, I was taken with my family from our home in Bedford Park to Liverpool Street by 'four-wheeler' – which meant a horse-drawn carriage – but later we were only taken as far as Shepherd's Bush Underground Station and then went by Central Line to Liverpool Street. Trains were all steam-powered then, even the underground ones, and stations were entirely covered in soot. Light hardly penetrated the windows of the trains or the roof of the main station and everything stank horribly.

My mother had a personal travelling chest-of-drawers, similar to those used by colonial travellers, made of canvas-covered wood with leather corner pieces. The weight must have been considerable, but fortunately all our luggage was yanked about by porters, so she did not have to carry it herself. We would travel Second Class, often booking a whole compartment for the family plus maids. Compared with First Class seats, which were well-upholstered and had clean cloths on the backs and arms, the Second Class seats were narrow and pretty hard, although moderately clean. The Third Class carriages, however, had slatted wooden benches and were very grimy, with spit all over the floor, particularly in the smoking compartments.

Once we got to Norfolk we found that the rolling stock which served the country stations and local towns on the eastern side of England was decidedly primitive. Corridors did not exist or were extremely rare. Carriages were divided into compartments with a door at each side. At any station, either door could be opened, so you had to make sure before you got out that you were on the right side of the train for the platform. Each door had a heavy glass window held in position by a leather strap pierced with holes and fixed onto a brass knob. The only handle to open the door was on the outside, so first you had to lower the window in its thick wooden frame by hauling on the strap to free it from the brass knob. Then, in mounting panic that the train would move off before you could do it, you had to lean out of the window and open the door by the outside handle.

Inside, the benches faced each other each holding four or – at a pinch – five people. A string net was supported on iron brackets over each seat for bags and coats and a chain ran along one wall, operating an alarm to stop the train in an emergency (there was a £5 fine for false alarms). There was generally a framed map of the locality, a mirror and a local poster or advertisement on the other wall of the compartment. We were advised to avoid resting our heads against anything as lice and ringworm were very prevalent.

Intermediate stations along the line were manned by a stationmaster who also worked the signals, and at times he served as a porter as well. Infrequent as they were, trains then provided the major means of transport, so there was always a great deal of luggage and quantities of parcels were carried in the guard's van.

At some mainline stations, you could buy a 'picnic basket' which consisted of a wicker basket with rolls and butter, perhaps with a piece of chicken on a cardboard plate. This was a great boon as there was no access to a buffet carriage. However, Mother often brought along a picnic from home. On one train journey my mother was sitting next to my father (who always sat with his back to the engine to avoid the danger of smuts or bits of grit being blown into his eyes) and she had brought a picnic basket to share between them. When they had eaten their sandwiches and hard-boiled eggs, my father put the shells back in the wrapping paper. My mother, always ready to take charge of a situation, said "Give it to me, dear. I will deal with it". She put all the scraps together and threw the packet out of the window. Unfortunately, she cast it in the direction the train was travelling. The result was that it re-entered the open window with some force and burst open against the chest of a gentleman who was sitting opposite Papa.

An embarrassing moment for Mother

Apparently he remained quite rigid and utterly silent, while my mother had to stand over him picking off the bits of broken eggshell and crumbs which covered his coat. In spite of her somewhat formidable appearance, in her firmly-laced bodice and large elegant hat, my mother was always ready to see the funny side of things and had on this occasion a fierce struggle to maintain her dignity.

Eleven

Kirby Green – Our House in Norfolk

After our train journey we finally arrived at the house in Norfolk and then our holiday really began. Kirby Green was very old and had great charm, and its front entrance appeared in more than one of my father's paintings. He designed and had made quite an elaborate wooden porch with seats on either side of the front door, screened by lattice work which supported a climbing rose.

The outside of the house, like that of several neighbouring cottages, was originally a timber frame filled in with what was called 'wattle' and a great deal of clay dug from a pit near the house. (This pit, beyond the driveway and the field or paddock, had later been filled with water and was by now a very large pond or, if you looked at it another way, a very small lake). At some point our house had then been faced with mellow brick.

The walls inside the house were hollow and at the appropriate season we could hear the scurry and scuffle of the rodent population who had fled there from the nearby fields during harvest time. There was an enormous, thick stone chimney between the dining room and the stone-floored kitchen. These parts of the building must have formed the original house, to which the entrance passage and sitting room had been added later. A winding stair with uneven steps was built round the chimney. Upstairs, the floors were of massive oak planks on huge beams still showing their axe marks.

*Papa's painting of the Norfolk house:
the porch appeared in many of his paintings*

Beyond the kitchen was a large larder-cum-butter-house with its own pump and well. The brick-paved floor sloped to a shallow drain so the floor could be sluiced down. This drain very probably led the water back to the well, the only source of drinking water for the house.

In the country there was no water laid on. In most country houses it had to be pumped by hand from a well in the garden, although some had a well sited beneath the kitchen sink and could draw water up there. My parents invested in a big earthenware filter which was filled with our well-water drawn up by a pump. The pump, in a sort of iron cradle, was positioned over a trough in which receptacles could be placed. Water was forced out of a great spout by the action of the pump and the trough functioned as a sink and general washing area.

There were no taps in the country house!
One of our maids had to pump water into the trough

Only cold water came out of the pump, however: all our hot water had to be obtained from a coal-fired boiler called a 'copper' situated in a lean-to scullery leading out of the kitchen. The scullery contained a big brick coal bunker and beside it stood the copper, built into a brick surround with its own fire chamber below. Next to that was a very old bread oven, also made of brick. We did not use this large oven, which had a draught vent opening into it from below and a chimney above. In the past it had been heated up by a wood fire which had actually been lit inside it. When the oven reached the required temperature the embers were scooped out, the floor of the oven was quickly swept, and bread dough was placed directly on the hot brick floor of the oven to bake. However, the only light for the scullery was the upper half of a stable-type door – when open – so it was not an ideal place to work.

Doing the laundry was hot work, standing next to the copper in the scullery

Another bread oven was later built in beside the kitchen range in the kitchen itself, but the heat for that oven was obtained from burning wood in a compartment below it. Cook was occasionally persuaded to bake bread in it and the loaves produced by this method were always far better than any modern ones. The extreme heat gradually reducing as the fire died down made the crusts golden-brown, while the bread inside was quite delicious.

I remember electricity being installed at our house in London, but in the country we only had oil lamps in the main rooms. The light they gave was quite pleasant but they had to have their wicks trimmed and they had to be refilled with oil every day. For other rooms, like bedrooms, candles were needed, and holders with handles (and rims to catch the dripping wax) were kept ready for use. We would take one with us if we visited an unlit part of the house at night.

There were no electric irons in the country house, so all the ironing was

Our maid would judge how hot the iron was by holding it near her face

done with flat irons. These were heated on the kitchen stove (which was kept polished by applications of black-lead) or they were stood against a lighted grate. Both were rather dirty places, so the base of the iron had to be wiped clean after each re-heating. Some people had a kind of shoe which fitted over the iron. The shoe was removed during heating, but put back on again when the iron was hot enough to press the clothes.

Taking baths was very primitive in country areas at that time, where most of the houses had no indoor plumbing of any kind. Keeping me clean was quite a complicated affair. The saucer-bath which had been such a helpful part of our luggage was placed on a large Turkish towelling square on the nursery floor, and near it were a couple of three-gallon cans of water – one hot and the other cold. These were poured

My saucer-bath was put on the nursery floor, waiting to be filled with water from the three-gallon cans

in and mingled to the correct temperature, and I would then sit in the bath to be soaped all over and rinsed down with a large sponge.

This rustic mode of bathing applied to guests, too (and we did have guests in Norfolk – our London friends Sir Frank Dicksee and his sister, for example, often came to stay). A similar form of tub was issued daily in the mornings to the visitors in their own rooms, although, of course, they were not given the same personal supervision which I enjoyed. The

Our poor maids! The stairs were so steep and the water-cans were very heavy

maids had to carry the heavy jugs of water up the steep stairs and then later, while the family breakfasted, they had to empty the saucer-baths into pails and carry the dirty water downstairs again. To ease their load, my father, who was a born inventor, had a hole knocked in one of the first floor walls and a kind of chute made, to flow into an outside drain.

There were outside lavatories – separate ones for the family and the maids. The only light in these lavatories came from a gap over the doorway. In each lavatory was a bench seat with holes in it and set below the holes were buckets, known as soil pans, which could be removed through a hatch at the back of the privy. The gardener's first job, at about seven o'clock in the morning, was to collect the soil pans from both lavatories and cart them down the garden. The contents were then buried in a pre-dug trench in an adjacent field.

The lavatory had more than one hole in the bench seat, so you could go to the loo with a friend if you liked!

It was in connection with these lavatories that my friend Greta and I once got into trouble.

I had first met Greta in London. She was eighteen months older than me and went to the school where I had my dancing lessons, but I did not know her very well at first. Then one day when Greta was ten her father, a charming, cultured young man who was a stockbroker or something in the City, suddenly become ill with typhoid fever and died only a few days later. His widow, Greta's mother, was Swedish and had originally come to England as a girl to be a governess to a family called the Aberdeens. By now, as well as Greta, she had a son aged twelve, another daughter aged five and she was expecting her fourth baby.

My mother was always ready to help anyone in trouble, and when she became aware of this neighbouring family in great distress she was determined to do something. She had all the children with us for the day of the funeral, and then invited Greta to spend two weeks with us when we went up to Norfolk during the summer holidays. This began a friendship which endured for the rest of our lives. For the first time I had a companion with whom I felt really secure. We never quarrelled, but every day, after lunch, we would wrestle like young puppies, exercising our muscles and laughing the whole time, much to the amusement of my parents.

This visiting for about two weeks every year became a pattern, and bitterly did I miss her when the time came for her to go home!

One year when Greta was staying with us, she and I were set on learning Morse code, and it was in connection with our Morse signalling that we found out something interesting about the outdoor lavatories. We discovered that the two seemingly separate loos, one for the owners of the house and one for the servants, although carefully approached by different routes, were actually side by side. We found we could tap Morse messages through the separating wall. However, in the end this activity was strictly forbidden, because it upset the personal routines of both family and staff.

Another thing I always connect with Greta is making ice cream. Ice cream was an unknown luxury to us, but once when she was staying it was decided we should make some. A block of plain ice was ordered and brought out from either Beccles or Bungay. It came in a large brick and was broken up and put in a kind of barrel with an inner drum which held, I think, pure cream and mashed-up strawberries. There was a handle to turn and I remember it was taken out into the orchard, where Greta and I had to turn it until it froze. It took about an hour. I still remember the wonderful taste of the ice cream we made that day.

Greta and me, wondering what we will get up to next

Twelve

Our Garden and the Big Outdoors

I HAVE MENTIONED THE GARDENER, so now I really must tell you about the garden. Ever since her childhood, my mother had loved and cared for plants and my father enjoyed including them in his paintings, so together my parents began to enlarge and beautify the garden at Kirby Green. It was about two acres in size and had been rather neglected. Both my parents enjoyed tennis and my brother excelled at all sports, so under Mother's management the garden soon boasted a large, well-kept tennis court and croquet lawn as well as a fine herbaceous border and, in the orchard area, a small pond with water plants. Farm horses put out to grass in the adjacent field used to drink at this pond, but my parents had it cleaned out and deepened and a narrow path made round it. Soon it contained newts and queer water insects we could fish for, while its banks were made into an alpine garden with plants cascading down over large rocks.

When my mother first started to improve the garden she took on a young man whose father ran the local pub. At first it was a matter of digging and clearing under her instruction, but before long he was able to undertake the care of the garden unsupervised. His name was Pumfrey, and Papa actually used him as a model in a painting called *The Shadow*.

Eventually Pumfrey left to take over the pub from his father, and we then had a series of characters as gardeners who came and went. One was old Garny. Mother asked him one day what his real name was, as sometimes he was called 'Jeremy', sometimes 'Germany' and so on.

"Well, Ma'am," he replied, "I don't rightly know. You see, I can't read or write, so sometimes I am called this and sometimes that"!

After a few other gardeners we at last had a more permanent one called Tom, a youth of about sixteen, who was both willing and intelligent. His uncle was an experienced gardener who used to come during the week to supervise and train him. Tom would also groom the pony and the donkey, having caught them (no mean task!), and sometimes drive the trap to collect things from the station. Occasionally he would also drive us to the river or to the local town so that he could either stable or guard the pony while we shopped. He had a rather individual way of dressing: he thought it looked smart to wear a 'dicky' (a stiff, white false shirt front), but whereas most men would wear such an item tucked into their jacket to look like the front of a starched shirt, Tom was not aware of this and for smart occasions would invariably appear with it outside his coat.

I had my own small, netted fruit garden and took great pride in growing gooseberries, currants and every sort of soft fruit. I would pick them and take them into Cook to make into jam, and she was always ready to oblige. As we had an extensive and varied orchard, fruit was plentiful and jam was always on the boil. This attracted wasps from far and near, and they came in buzzing swarms. The maids would put sugar and water in jam-jars covered with perforated paper and hang them outside the kitchen window and door. In a very short time the jars were almost filled with the black and yellow bodies of the trapped wasps.

Wasps were such a nuisance that we often felt obliged to destroy their nests. I (and sometimes my brother as well) used to go out at sundown with Fred Morris, the neighbouring farmer, and watch the wasps' homeward flight. They could be clearly seen against some dark background. We tracked their route by noting the points they passed until we were led to what looked like a small fountain of wasps, which was the wasps descending into a hole in the ground. Once this was located Mr Morris would produce a bottle of cyanide and pour it into the hole. The effect was immediate and we could see the wasps drop dead as they arrived on the spot.

The next morning we would return to the nest and Fred Morris, armed with a spade, would dig it out. Very rarely were there any surviving wasps, but the nests themselves were things of great beauty. Formed of several tiers of round, plate-like platforms, they were made of masticated wood pulp in varying shades of colour. Each nest was shaped like a football, smaller at the top and bottom and encased in flakes of wood pulp. The grubs inside were in individual cells, covered in a paper-like membrane. I once kept a tier, thinking it too lovely to be destroyed, only to find that after a couple of days the grubs emerged as fully-developed wasps. That was not such a good idea!

As well as wasps there were several hornets' nests in the area. Most of them were in hollow trees but there was once one hanging from the rafters of an open shed on the farm. We did not investigate that one too closely. One summer there was even a swarm of bees clustered on a branch of the big ash tree which stood in our garden. Our gardener at that time was a handsome old man called Becket. Tall, bearded and and powerful, although then in his seventies, he must have been quite remarkable in his youth. When consulted about the bees, he at once said, "I can deal with that". Next day he appeared in a hat and veil, with a bucket, a trowel and a long ladder which he leant against the branch where the swarm was hanging.

With evident delight in having an audience, he mounted the ladder,

Becket climbed up the ladder to deal with the bees while Mother and I looked on admiringly

held out the bucket and drove the trowel deep into the hanging swarm. The bees dropped two feet, but then the law of 'what goes up must come down' was reversed for, having come down, they rose up - inside his trouser legs! Becket's descent was spectacular: with a loud roar and a look of horror he came down that ladder like a fireman on call, and ran a three-minute mile across the paddock and into the pond. He survived. Meanwhile, the whole air was alive with angry bees and everyone was running wildly out of reach, including the donkey and pony. A couple of bees got stuck in my mother's hair and I had considerable difficulty in picking them out. She was stung twice, but not too badly.

I can't remember what eventually happened to the bees. I think that Fred Morris might have come quietly the next day and collected them by enclosing them in a sack, but I was certainly well out of the way.

We had lots of space to play in and some excellent secret places outside the house in Norfolk. In the garden was the immense ash tree where the bees had once swarmed. One day my brother enlarged a small opening in the trunk and found that the tree was hollow. While I lay among the hollow roots with one of our cousins, Eric and another cousin cut away a great deal of the rotten core, to make a space as big as a room inside the tree. He then made a small door and covered it with bark so the entrance hole would be unnoticeable. This secret hideaway became a great joy and was much used. Once, when the local scout troop had just been formed, my parents gave a tea party for them and during the party thirteen large lads were able to get inside the tree together, standing upright.

Another secret place was inside the summer house at the end of the croquet lawn. The summer house was built of pine planks still covered in their bark and inside it was lined with smoothly planed tongue-and-groove planking. It had a half-glazed door and two windows which overlooked the adjoining fields. One summer when Greta was with us, my father showed us a panel inside the summer house that could be pushed up to reveal a little cupboard. According to local gossip, this was for holding the liquid refreshment belonging to the farm steward who had once lived in our house. He had been able to come and 'relax' in the summer house whilst still watching the labourers at work in the fields from his position near the windows.

The croquet lawn where Eric and I sometimes played

On the opposite side of the croquet lawn was an enormous barn with a concrete floor where on wet days we could knock a ball against the walls. If my brother was at home and he felt so inclined, he could fix up an elaborate swing from the heavy rafters.

I used to spend hours fishing in the small pond in the garden, which had a great variety of water life. I would fill an old tin bathtub with my catch and sit for a long time watching their reactions to each other, but there was no-one to ask about wildlife. However, I had just learnt to read and one day found a book on the dining room bookshelf all about plants and animals, which I took down and struggled through from cover to cover. It stirred a lasting interest for me in the natural world: it was Darwin's *Voyage of the Beagle*.

As to plants, there was a wonderful variety of wild flowers in the surrounding fields, which I loved to pick. I was given a flower-drying frame and an exercise book, and with the help of two excellent books on native flora, I amassed a considerable knowledge of the local flowers.

The pond at the front of the house

The great pond or small lake I mentioned before, which lay between our field and the farm, was another good place to have fun. When I was young my brother even built a small island in it, which became the focus for many childhood games of make-believe. On one occasion Greta and I held a party on it, for which we dressed up in my parents' clothes. I put on long skirts and Greta, who was taller than me, looked really quite impressive in an old suit of my father's. She even snipped bits from under the pony's mane to provide a fine moustache.

The pond was large enough to take a boat. My father and Eric, who was then about twenty-five, were both good at carpentry and between them they made a boat which we called a punt and launched it onto the pond. (In fact, a proper punting technique was not feasible because over the years the pond had filled up so much with mud it was impossible to extract a pole: we had to propel the punt with a paddle instead). The punt had buoyancy compartments at either end which acted as seats and although it was very wobbly, it never overturned. The sides and bottom were painted in hot pitch in an attempt to make them waterproof, but this was only partially successful, so we became pretty expert with the baler.

There was also a very old rowing-boat we could use, but it leaked so badly that, if you did not bale furiously, the water was over your ankles before you reached the other side of the pond.

One summer, in about 1913 or 1914, there was a bad drought and the big pond almost dried up. The thick, evil-smelling mud, three to four feet deep, was exposed, and there were only very shallow pools of water remaining in the bottom. In these, large golden carp flapped, exhausted, in their last throes of life, as well as huge eels (one of which, when measured, was found to be over three foot long and as thick as a man's arm). My father organised a working party which included my brother, the gardener and one or two others. They dug out as much mud as possible and managed to saved some of the fish by transferring them to deeper water in the parts newly dug out. Some of the mud they dug out was useful – young willow trees were planted and the mud was put behind them to enlarge the small island and to extend the landing stage.

There were so many special places I loved at the Norfolk house, but for sheer beauty I would go in the evenings to the stile beyond the summer house, where I could look over the fields and watch beautiful sunsets. The sky would shade from blue to green, the fleecy clouds would be pink with the last rays of the evening light and I could see the silhouette of our local Norman church, which stood outlined against the glow.

There were other places to enjoy beyond the house and garden, of course. About two and a half miles down the hill from our village, Kirby Green, and beyond the village of Kirby Cane, ran the river Waveney, on which heavy wherries carried grain and other produce. It wound through the the marshes between Beccles and Bungay and the locks at Ellingham and Geldeston. We kept a rowing boat at Ellingham Mill and would go there by governess cart to use it, leaving Jack or Kitty stabled in a nearby outbuilding.

Boating was always fun

My aunt wore an amazing bathing-dress

We younger ones even used to swim in the river and the mill pond. The water ran with considerable force and I was rather scared, but I loved to swim down the river behind the boat, with my father at the oars. Of course, swimming costumes in those days were rather cumbersome, often made of wool and always very decorous, covering the whole torso (no bikinis for us!). I can still picture with amazement the outfit worn by young Uncle Frank's wife: a heavy blue serge bathing-dress with a full knee-length skirt. It was a sight to see, and so was her unique swimming action. We knew she had double-jointed hands, but she must also have had an extra hinge in her back, for she glided through the water like a swan with not only her head, but part of her shoulders well out of the water. How she managed this in her extraordinary costume I cannot imagine: water-logged, it must have weighed a ton.

We often saw cousins and other relations of ours who lived in the neighbourhood. My family delighted in picnics on the river, often shared with members of the other families. Picnics then were not at all the light-hearted affairs they are today, but meals which involved complicated preparation. Food, plates, cloth and cutlery were packed in a large hamper and there was a separate tin container for the kettle and the methylated stove on which it was to be boiled. As I grew older it became my job to wash the picnic dishes before they were packed up to go home, and this had to be done in the river. It was a messy business which I loathed. I had to get a footing among the reeds and riverside plants and then use a mop to clean the plates with cold river water, helped out with any hot water left in the kettle.

One thing I must say about our time spent in Norfolk: it was mercifully more or less free from walks. We sometimes just walked up to the village, but that was quite fun because the road had no footpath, only tracks like sheep-tracks worn up and down the banks by children on their way to school (which made the pedestrian route much more interesting than the straight road). The school was at a crossroads about halfway between our house and the village and was entirely run by an elderly woman called Mrs. Holland. She was somewhere in her sixties at the time we knew her, tall and gaunt with huge sorrowful eyes. Although she may not have been inspiring to look at, however, she did get results with simple basic education and good manners.

We would follow the children's sheep-tracks on the way to the village

Thirteen

GOING FURTHER AFIELD

APART FROM OCCASIONALLY WALKING to the village, I either played in the garden or was taken for rides in the old governess cart drawn by dearest Jack. Nanny learned to drive it, but it was very noisy to travel in because the iron-bound wheels made a shattering din.

My mother had a much smarter job with highly-polished woodwork, upholstered seats with backs and new-fangled rubber tyres. Both her little cart and the governess cart were entered by a small door at the back, which had a step to get up to it. The driver and passengers then sat on seats at either side which faced into the carriage. If you wanted to see where you were going (which the driver usually needed to do!) then you had to use a sideways dorsal twist to face the front.

To go as far afield as Beccles or Bungay we generally hired a landau (a four-wheeled carriage) from the local publican, Pumfrey Senior, our gardener's father. This Pickwickian figure would drive us himself, but unfortunately he did rather enjoy his drink and on one occasion arrived at our house in a state of near coma. It was entirely thanks to the horse that he had reached the house at all! He was soon sobered up by my mother's pointed reprimand, but a few years later he finally succumbed to his intake and had to leave the public house. It was for this reason that his son, young Pumfrey, finally stopped being our gardener. He married a charming wife and took over from his father as publican.

Mr. Pumfrey would drive us in the landau

In matters of transport young Pumfrey was more up-to-date, and when the local squire bought a new car he purchased the squire's old one and also hired himself out to drive people places. The car was an early Humber, originally painted red, which had faded to a strange orange colour. It was very high off the ground and gave one a good view over most hedges. There was a seat beside the driver and a sofa-shaped seat for two at the back. As a great treat I was allowed to go with my parents in this vehicle as far as Norwich. My cousin Ted, aged about thirteen, was visiting us, and he and I had to sit on camp stools in front of the back seat. That was all right when the road was straight but it was pretty risky going round corners, as the roads were not cambered and the low sides of the car offered little protection.

Road surfaces were only water-bound macadam, mud or stones. Heaps of fresh stones were left shot down beside the road, and an old roadman spent his time sitting on the piles, breaking up the stones with a hammer and filling the potholes caused by passing farm wagons and the very rare passage of an early car. If a car did pass in the summertime it would always raise a choking cloud of white dust, blotting vision and completely covering the hedges and verges. It smothered pedestrians and passengers alike, so women wore special clothes for motoring: dust-coats and veils which could be pulled over their faces. It was obligatory to honk the horn at every crossroads and when my parents had hired the Humber and gone to Beccles, I could stand in the far corner of the garden and hear them coming home from a good mile and a half away.

Eric had some friends, three young men and a girl, who lived nearby at Broome Place. Being very up-to-date, their father bought a new Sunbeam. Not content with being a passenger, he was determined to watch the speedometer and supervise the driver, so he had the body of the car specially built to allow him to do that. A kind of armchair enclosed in glass was put next to the chauffeur's seat, so that the master had a clear view of the controls.

The master himself was so much the living image of Edward VII, who was on the throne at the time, that when I was shown his photograph I mistook it for one of the king. His family was delighted and said, "Oh, Father will be pleased!" His wife looked exactly like Queen Victoria and their whole lifestyle seemed built on the resemblance. The father would not permit his chauffeur to drive at more than twenty-five miles per hour, but one day when Eric was in the Sunbeam with one of the sons he realised that they were going much faster than that. Later, he questioned the chauffeur, who giggled and said that the speed restriction was easily fiddled: he had set the speedometer so that the needle never went above twenty-five! The car was probably travelling at about fifty miles an hour, which in those days was quite a reckless speed.

Of course, we also rode bicycles if we wanted to get about in Norfolk. The bicycle I first used had no freewheel mechanism, so unless I pedalled it stopped dead, which was rather alarming. The next bicycle was a pretty basic model which had almost the opposite problem. It had no brakes, so in order to slow down I had to contort my legs and grip the front wheel between my feet. My brother had taken me out for my first ride on it, I might say, without having told me how to make it stop!

I had to stop the bicycle by gripping the front wheel between my feet

When I was about twelve I used to cycle over to our local vicarage, about three and a half miles, to take flowers to the vicar's wife. The rector of our parish was a dear old man called Darwin Fox (I believe he was the nephew of the famous naturalist whose book I had read so avidly). His wife was crippled with gout, so they used to tour the district in a pony chaise called a victoria – a cross between a carriage and a bath-chair – the only transport which it was possible for the poor old lady to climb in and out of. They always made a ceremonial call once during our summer stay in Norfolk. The victoria would stop on the road a short distance from the house and we often used to go out to Mrs. Fox to have a chat if she was unable to walk from the carriage to see us.

Every summer the old couple gave a party for the village children and word would be sent, "Could Sophie please come to help?" I used to set off on my bicycle, clutching all the old tennis racquets and balls I could find, and while old Mrs. Fox sat, wrapped up, in an armchair on a kind of verandah, I would organise and play games with about a dozen children. I never minded doing this because the old people were so grateful.

If you remember, I had two aunts who were called Nellie, one on my father's side and one on my mother's. My mother's sister was known as

It was quite a chore for Big Aunt Nellie's daughters to pull her along

'Big Aunt Nellie' and she lived with her husband at Beccles, about five miles from our house in Norfolk. Their three eldest children were much the same age as my brother (although the fourth was an 'afterthought', only six and a half years older than me) and they used to row their boat the seven miles from Beccles or meet us halfway at Geldeston Lock to join in boating picnics on the river Waveney. They would also cycle over for tennis parties and I remember on one occasion when Big Aunt Nellie and her daughters were expected over for tea I went a little way along the road to meet them. To my amazement, they were taking turns to pull her in a kind of wicker Bath chair adapted to fit behind a bicycle. She was no light weight and the distance covered was at least five miles, so this was no mean feat.

Fourteen

Local Life in Kirby

Although we were far from London when in Norfolk, we were not completely out of touch with our family, or indeed with our other life. My father's paper, for example, was delivered every morning at about ten o'clock by our local stationmaster. It would be delivered by train to the station and then the stationmaster would bicycle with it two and a half miles up the hill to us. He said that he enjoyed coming because my father nearly always met him at the gate and they had a chat about all kinds of subjects. I presume that on the same trip he also delivered a morning paper to the Squire.

In fact, we were always exchanging visits with friends and relations living nearby and inviting guests and young relations from London to join us on holiday while we were at Kirby Green. We also got to know some of the local people and see aspects of rural life at first hand. On the other side of the pond from our cottage was a farmhouse and the people who lived there were always kind and welcoming. The son of the family ran the farm and my brother spent many happy times with him, out rough shooting. As I got older I used to walk through the barnyard to visit the family. I was often allowed to help make the butter, turning the handle of the big wooden churn and then washing the butter in the shallow sink and patting it into oblong blocks.

It was hard work turning the handle of the big butter churn

I also enjoyed watching the milking, which was done by hand, and even took a turn myself now and again, but I was rather horrified by the conditions in which the cows were sometimes kept. In the byres the cattle dung (referred to as 'valuable manure') was allowed to pile up to a depth of about three feet and once a certain cow was coughing so much that I asked whether it was ill. I was told that it had 'the wasting disease', which I later discovered meant tuberculosis, or TB, a disease which can be passed to humans. (Not long after that, when I was about six and a half, I had to have the operation for tubercular glands which I mentioned before. It involved me staying in a nursing home with Nanny and then having to go to the seaside at Margate to recuperate.

Local Life in Kirby

I was even allowed to milk the cows myself sometimes

For a long time afterwards I had serious middle-ear trouble with agonising pain on occasions, and was considered to be delicate. However, the continual walking I was subjected to in my childhood must have strengthened me because in time I completely recovered.)

At harvest time the corn was scythed by hand and left in long rows to dry, then collected up into stooks to dry out further before being brought in. When the great wagons came in from the fields, piled high, I was sometimes lifted right up on top of the load or allowed to sit on the back of one of the magnificent carthorses. The village women and children would then come to 'glean' the ground. ('Gleaning' means picking up all the fallen grains on the ground, rather than letting them go to waste.) I used to see the gleaners pass, each with a bottle of cold tea and a bundle

It was fun to watch the corn being scythed

of food tied up in a red cotton kerchief and hung on the end of a stick over their shoulders. I tried to join in with gleaning, but was stopped by Mother, who pointed out that I did not need the corn and that if I took it I would be denying the poor.

As well as the farmers themselves, we also knew some of the labourers who worked on the farm. Old Charlie Crickmore was one of them and in the evening we would often meet him, in his labourer's smock and straw hat, lumbering home with somewhat erratic gait. He never failed to greet us with his wide grin and friendly twinkling eyes.

One day, standing on our side of the pond, I was watching Charlie and another man with the farmer. They were on top of a very high rick,

It really looked as if old Charlie Crickmore had drowned

almost at the edge of the barnyard on the further side of the pond. A certain amount of jovial banter was taking place when Charlie took a step backwards, lost his footing and plummeted into the pond. For what seemed ages, the only thing visible was Charlie's hat and pitchfork floating on the water. Eventually Charlie surfaced, crawled out and emerged through the hedge, to be met by a roar of raucous laughter from the watchers on the stack.

The wagons were loaded very high at harvest time.
Imagine riding on the top of all that!

So you see, generally the pace of life was pretty peaceful in the country, but occasionally we had our little diversions. One such for Nanny was funerals.

Kirby church, where local funerals were held, was not in the present village of Kirby, but some way out across the fields from it where an earlier village had once stood. (As in many parts of Norfolk, it was because of the Black Death in medieval times that our church had lost the village which originally surrounded it. The disease had taken such a heavy toll in the first settlement that the survivors had rebuilt their homes some way off to escape contamination, and the houses of the original village, having been built for the most part of wattle and daub, gradually rotted away and were lost in the surrounding fields). We could hear the sound of the bells from the old tower each Sunday, ringing out for matins and evensong, and sometimes the tolling of a single bell would echo across the fields to give notice of a funeral - one ring for a man, two for a woman, three for a child. Occasionally Nanny's curiosity would get the better of her and she would 'just happen' to be passing, with me in tow, at about the time of the funeral. I would stand, greatly intrigued, watching the small group waiting for the cortège to emerge. They would bring out large white cotton handkerchiefs with an inch-wide edging of black and raise them ceremoniously to their faces.

Another great excitement for us was the burglary which once took place at the cottage. Our house was really quite isolated, surrounded by fields and approached down a narrow lane from the main road about half a mile away. It was fully furnished, but mainly with old furniture my parents had picked up at sales or from small secondhand dealers, so we were surprised that burglars would be interested in it. Also, we lived in an area where everyone knew each other, so it came as a great shock to find we had been burgled.

It happened that at the time of the burglary my father had been expecting visitors, so he had laid in an unusually large supply of alcohol. Later, when we were all out the burglars had got into the house. Apparently they had little difficulty in entering the cottage and, having moved things around a bit while searching, they discovered my father's alcohol supply in a cupboard under the stairs. They seized a large silk carriage rug and, using it like a sling, filled it with as many bottles of whisky and other spirits as they could. They then left, no doubt looking for somewhere to hide their loot, but as they were sampling it generously on their way, they ended up in a ditch not far from the house. (Because they were unused to drinking anything stronger than beer, the spirits seem to have had a devastating effect.)

Interestingly, the local policeman had also been involved in sampling the drinks, so when my father came to investigate the burglary he found our constable suffering the after-effects as much as the burglars. Although I can't remember the outcome of all this, I do remember my mother bemoaning the loss of the fine silk rug she had been given by a wealthy relation.

Fifteen

Canning Fruit: our bit for the war effort

The Great War was a time of excitement in the village. On the 4th August 1914 war was declared and four days later my brother had joined the Volunteer Army and was sent to train with the Royal Garrison Artillery. For us in Norfolk there was a great commotion in the village when soldiers were billeted at the Manor. Tents were set out for the troops and horse lines laid out in the grounds. Many of the volunteer soldiers were wealthy men and brought their own horses: one brought a stud of fourteen! The officers were accommodated comfortably enough in the Manor House but the other ranks had no access to creature comforts. When my parents found that some of these were educated men, doctors and the like, they were invited to our home for baths – presumably taken in slipper baths in the spare room.

During the war our own family life carried on as before, with the summer months spent at Kirby, but sometimes we heard the far-off sounds of bombardment over in Belgium or the strange clanking sound of a German Zeppelin passing overhead.

At this time the effects of submarine warfare and loss of manpower caused grave shortages. As it became increasingly necessary to produce and preserve home-grown fruit and vegetables, Women's Institutes all over the country organised canning demonstrations. ('Canning' was a process where produce could be sealed into sterilised containers, usually jars, but occasionally tins. It was then supposed to keep well for several years.) Our village had a very active Women's Institute and when my mother attended one of their meetings in the local Working Men's Club she saw the possibility of taking some of our plentiful fruit supply back to London. I was about fourteen then and had gone with her to the demonstration.

Mother realised that bottling would not be suitable for us, as glass jars were heavy and easily broken, but tins were another matter. We were shown the whole process of sterilisation and sealing with a soldering iron and told we could order the whole kit in time for the coming harvest. Accordingly an order was placed, although there was a slight hesitation when my mother found that the minimum number of tins which could be ordered at any time was one gross (which meant 144 tins!).

My father undertook to do the soldering, without any previous experience, and I too was eager to take part in the experiment. An enormous wooden crate, about four foot square and of similar height, was subsequently delivered and when we opened it we found it full of gleaming tin cans packed in straw, with a book of instructions and various implements needed for the canning process. These included long-handled pincers, rather like a pair of scissors with twin half-circles, to grip the tins, a tube of 'flux' which mystified us, sticks of tin solder known as 'tinning' and, I think, an outsize soldering iron.

One of the instructions we read was that the tins had to be immersed in boiling water for a specified length of time to sterilise them. However, to bring eight gallons of water to the boil in the copper in the scullery always took a considerable time so the first job was to light the fire beneath the clothes boiler and coax it into a roaring blaze. Meanwhile the apples, pears, plums and any other available fruit had to be prepared and then stewed in large jam pans on the kitchen stove, which also needed to be well stoked.

The crate (taking up considerable space) had been put in the kitchen, and tins had to be taken from it and dropped into the water, which by now was boiling and bubbling. Once they were sterilised they had to be taken out and filled with fruit, and it was a great sport to insert the pincers into the steam and clutch at the tins, one by one. Each time I gripped a tin, I ran with it to the kitchen for Cook to ladle in boiling fruit and liquid. No sugar was used because none could be spared. The tins were filled to within one-eighth of an inch of the top and the lid was then placed into position.

Each lid had to be sealed all around its edge immediately. In the centre of each lid was a small hole to allow the steam to escape, but directly the edges were completed this was also sealed with a dab of solder. The soldering iron had to be ready, heated red-hot in the open grate of the kitchen stove and primed with tinning. If the iron was too hot, the tinning would melt and slip off it, which meant it would then have to be 're-tinned', but if it were not hot enough the solder would not melt sufficiently to run around the preimeter of the lid. I soon learned to solder so my father and I could work as a team. Failures were few but they were dramatic: the fruit in cans which had been poorly sealed would ferment, and eventually the whole tin would explode!

Sixteen

THE EDUCATION I HAD ALWAYS LONGED FOR

EVERY YEAR WHEN SUMMER WAS OVER we had to go back to London, and the day when we had to row the boat back seven miles to the boat-builder's yard in Beccles always marked the end of our stay in Norfolk. I had to go to school and my father had to return to his studio, while my mother took up her London social life again. I was at Miss Dolman's school until I was fourteen, but during the war I began attending St. Paul's School in Turnham Green.

It was because of my dear friend Greta that I finally gained at least some formal education at St. Paul's. When she had been to stay with us and I had still been at the age for playing with dolls, she took always a medical rather than a maternal interest in them. In the games we played I was always the mother and she was the doctor. She even once carried out a surgical operation on one which happened to have a stuffed body. Looking back now I can see that these games were clearly shades of things to come.

Greta was not only clever but very hardworking and after her father's death she was awarded a scholarship to St Paul's School. I longed to go there too, and after much nagging and pleading managed to extract from my father a grudging promise that I could go there when I had attained the enormous age of fourteen. As I neared the magic age I firmly reminded my father of his promise. He was a person whose word was his bond so, although he did not altogether like it, he finally said yes.

When Miss Dolman was told she was aghast and declared that I should never get in because I had not been taught any arithmetic and could not possibly pass the entrance exam. Of course, because of my afternoon walks and my dancing lessons on Saturdays I had never been at school at the times when the infamous Miss Ratty gave her arithmetic classes. However, I was not to be put off, and said, "The only thing is for me to have private coaching. Can't I have Miss Ratty?"

So Miss Ratty came, and charming and kind she turned out to be, not at all the harridan she appeared at school. She did her very best and I worked and worked. Greta was anxious for me to get in and when she saw some of the old-fashioned arithmetic which I had been taught, she came along and showed me newer methods.

The date of the entrance exam was after the time of my parents' annual summer migration to Norfolk, so that it was arranged that I should stay with Greta's family and that she should take me up to the school with her. I found the papers pretty hard, but in my oral interview the fact that I was really more at home with adults than with my contemporaries proved a blessing. I explained to the assistant headmistress of the school about my lack of arithmetic instruction and she was very kind. Some weeks later the notice arrived saying that I had passed the entrance exam.

The Education I had always longed for

I finally persuaded my parents to let me attend a proper school

Once at St Paul's I felt that I had finally succeeded in entering a proper school, but I still had problems. I was put in the lowest section of the form and found the other girls a pretty uninteresting lot. Some were actually rather horrid and others only interested in boys, but the teaching was good. I worked really hard and after getting top marks for a whole week, I accosted the assistant headmistress and told her I wanted to be moved up. She told me that was not possible, because I had never learnt any Latin. I replied that, in that case, I wanted to learn it and marched off to the headmistress herself. The other girls were scared stiff of Miss Grey but as I had lived almost entirely with people of her age, I found her less formidable. She was very surprised, and I was told once again that my mother had particularly asked that I should be placed in a low form to avoid being put under pressure. Oh dear! Such kindness, but so frustrating!

By then the war had begun and after a while there came the threat of bombing. Nightly air raids deprived us of sleep and my parents feared that I would be trapped during the daytime raids on my way to and from school at Turnham Green. Suddenly, I was told that I was to be sent away to a boarding school near Bexhill, where Biddy Lutyens had been. My mother took me to view the establishment, and we met the headmistress in the drawing room and were taken to see a largish bedroom I would be sharing with three others.

At this school I found I got on quite well with the other girls, quite a mixed lot, and with the assistant mistress, who was clever and still young. I also made friends with the French mistress, who found that I could understand her language well enough for her to be able to chat with me. However – oh dear! – my mother had not been shown anything below stairs. The classroom was reasonable and led onto the back garden, but the washroom and loo were primitive in the extreme and shared with the cook and the maid. The single, very thin, hand towel provided for them and twenty-four girls was neither hygienic nor funny, and on top of this

I suffered from terrible chilblains.

However, there were good points. The school was noted for its swimming and we used to bathe in the sea, even in quite rough weather. A special boat escorted us, rowed by an old man, and a raft was kept handy. The stronger swimmers, of whom I was one, used to swim to the quarter-mile buoy and back.

Sadly, by the time the war was drawing to an end, our charming assistant mistress left to get married and a perfect fool of a woman took her place. One night, the matron came to our room and woke me, saying that the headmistress wished to see me in her study. I was bewildered, being unaware of any problem. I found the Head standing with this new mistress, who launched into an accusation of insolence, bad behaviour and writing notes to other members of the class.

I was furious, said it was not true and stuck to my guns. The Head told the silly woman that I had been never known to lie and dismissed her from the room, while I was sent to fetch the rough book in which I had been making notes. The headmistress flipped through some pages and then suddenly roared with laughter. She had come across some caricatures I had drawn of the new teacher taking hockey practice. She asked if the mistress had seen the sketches, to which I answered, "Oh, no!"

"Well, make sure you never let her!" was the reply, "But, really, I can hardly scold you now that I have laughed, can I?" And that was the end of the matter.

The End of my Childhood

This is a picture I drew of myself: by this time I had "put up my hair" (which meant I had really become a young lady)

Tailpiece
The End of my Childhood

By the time the war was over I was sixteen, and although I was really rather young, my parents felt it best for me to leave school, 'put up my hair' and take part in social events with my cousins. Mother worried that, because our cousins were all several years older than me, I would miss out on social activities if I did not join in with the ones which were taking place at that time.

Amazingly, the war itself had not really affected my life in anything but minor ways. A favourite cousin had his health so damaged that I had to play endless games of croquet with him while the others enjoyed lively games of tennis, but luckily my brother had returned unscathed. We were in Norfolk when peace was declared, and my parents organised a great celebration lunch to which the entire village was invited. As we were some two miles out, our pony and donkey carts were used to carry the very young and very old to Kirby Green, and the villagers decorated the carts with coloured paper and flags. The feast was held in the great barn of the nearby farm and afterwards some of the men rendered their favourite songs. Then the idea was to have some dancing, for which I was to operate the gramophone (complete with large wooden horn), but as no-one danced I beat a hasty retreat.

We returned to Norfolk for a couple of summers after the war, but by then my father was already suffering from the illness which was to end his life. To me it was really the end of my childhood and my life in the future was to be very different in almost every way.

Afterword

Having have read Sophie's story to this point you may be interested to hear what happened to her when she was older. This section tells a little more of her life story and also explains how the book *Sophie: An Edwardian Childhood* came to be written.

The first thing to tell you is that Sophie's much-loved Papa, Edmund Blair Leighton, died in 1922 when Sophie was only twenty. He had been born in 1852, so by the time he was working on the fruit-canning with her in Norfolk during the First World War he was already quite an old father – in his sixties – and when he died he was seventy. Sadly, he did not live long enough to see what happened to Sophie in her adult life or to know that she followed in his footsteps and those of his father, training to be a professional painter.

From early childhood she had always drawn and painted for fun, but never expected to make a career of it. However, in the early 1920s after she left school she went on a sketching holiday which was also attended by one of her brother Eric's friends. This friend persuaded her that she really ought to take up painting as a serious activity, so after her father's death she studied for two years at the Slade School of Fine Art in Bloomsbury in London under a famous professor called Henry Tonks. As you can see from the line drawings and watercolour paintings reproduced in this book, Sophie was an accomplished artist, and although she spent many years of her young womanhood being a wife and mother and running a household, she later painted portraits professionally.

Not long after Sophie had finished her art training, she met a young civil engineer called Harold Harding who was working on the new Piccadilly Circus Underground Station. She became involved in helping him to

Aftreword

make a scale model of the Tube station, and all its associated services and tunnelling which was very complicated because of all the different levels, platforms, stairs and escalators. The model was a great success and it was on show for many years afterwards at the Science Museum in London.

Sophie and Harold became very fond of each other and in 1927 they were married. Sophie was twenty-five and Harold was twenty-seven. They went on to have three children, Caroline, Edmund and Robert. They travelled abroad a great deal in connection with Harold's work (he was a highly successful civil engineer who specialised in tunnelling) and Sophie drew and painted whenever she could – people, landscapes and still lifes.

Although Sophie lived until she was 93, and although I lived in the same small town as her in the last couple of years of her life, I never met her. However, I have met many people who knew her well, most notably her daughter Caroline Oboussier and Caroline's husband Philippe. I have also met Sophie's son Robert and his wife Lynnie.

When she was an old lady in her eighties, Sophie often recounted interesting tales of her childhood to her children and grandchildren. Eventually Caroline suggested she might like to write down some of her memories and illustrate the stories with a series of line-drawings and watercolours. Caroline and Lynnie Harding between them, with the aid of an electric typewriter, eventually created several copies of a small booklet for other members of the family to read. It contained many of the stories and pictures that are in this book, but Sophie's illustrations could only be reproduced in black and white because the booklet was a simple one made of folded photocopied sheets. Caroline and Lynnie entitled the booklet *Childhood Memories.*

About twenty years later, in 2007, Caroline transferred the typewritten material to her computer and also scanned in some of Sophie's pictures. However, although the watercolours were now reproduceable in colour, the picture quality was poor because the items Caroline scanned were only rather inferior colour photocopies of Sophie's originals.

Sadly, Caroline died some months later, and eventually Philippe Oboussier found himself in possession of one or two copies of *Childhood Memories*, various typewritten drafts which had been used in the booklet's compilation and Caroline's later computer files. It seemed that Caroline had been hoping to produce a properly-bound book with colour as well as black-and-white pictures.

Philippe set himself the task of finding the original pictures so that he might, finally, be able to produce such a book. A family search located all of them and Philippe also asked Sophie's son, Robert Harding, to find some relevant photographs of the young Sophie and her family, and of the houses in London and Norfolk where the Blair Leightons had lived during Sophie's childhood. Sophie's father had a very good camera and almost all of the photographs in this book were taken by him.

Finally, Philippe invited me to edit the various drafts and files of the text of Sophie's memoirs to produce a coherent whole. It was a great pleasure to take on such a task. When writing up *Childhood Memories*, Caroline and Lynnie had tended to improve on Sophie's writing style, perhaps finding her syntax over-simple, her rather idiosyncratic turns of phrase a little dated and her vocabulary insufficiently literary at times, but as far as possible I have tried to put each of Sophie's anecdotes back into the words of her earliest drafts. Sophie obviously had a keen sense of humour and even when writing as an old lady her youthful love of the ridiculous shines through, and it is often in charmingly child-like phrases that she expresses it.

I have gone one step further than Caroline and Lynnie, however, in that

AFTERWORD

a few phrases and passages of *Sophie: An Edwardian Childhood* are not in Sophie's words at all: they never existed in any of the original drafts. I wrote them myself, and I included them for two reasons; firstly, to help the shape of the book (so that one episode could flow smoothly into the next) and secondly, to help modern children understand various Edwardian or specialised concepts which Sophie took for granted when she was writing and therefore did not explain very clearly. After all, she was writing at the instigation of her grown-up daughter and daughter-in-law and probably had not thought of the final work as a children's book to be published in 2012.

Some of Sophie's own handwriting

127

Afterword

I would stress, however, that the proportion of text which has been written by me is very small indeed. I have tried at all times to keep my additions in a style similar to Sophie's and I certainly had a good model to follow. Sophie herself (despite a rather individualistic approach to spelling!) writes clearly and warmly about her early life and does not waste words. Her love of fun is paramount and we read of Jack the donkey and his antics, or Becket and the bee-swarm, as if we had been there to see them ourselves.

Of course, to some extent we can also *really* see them because of Sophie's lovely pictures, and it was to get the best reproductions of the originals that Philippe Oboussier invited book-designer Julia Harris to help in producing *Sophie: An Edwardian Childhood*. She has done a splendid job and I think the line drawings are as sharp and the watercolours as glowing as Sophie could have wished for. I hope you will read and re-read this book with as much pleasure as I have done.

Lily Neal
Topsham, 2012

Afterword

*Sophie in old age with her husband, Sir Harold Harding,
and the model they made during their courtship in the Twenties.*

My Family Tree

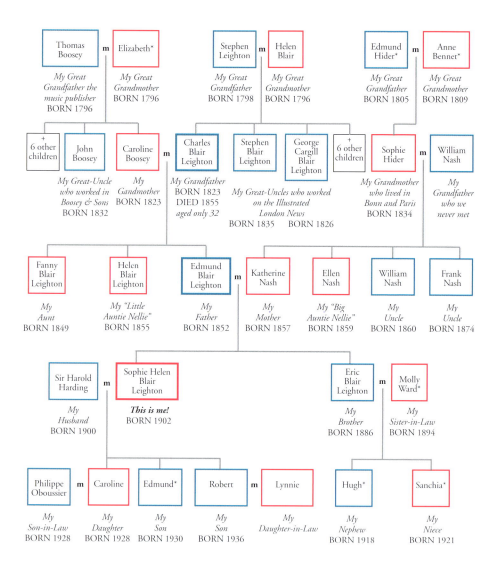

* Shows family members who are not mentioned in the text of this book.
m Shows people who were married to each other